TAKING JESUS SERIOUSLY

TAKING JESUS SERIOUSLY

The Teaching Of Jesus In Matthew

David Jackman

Christian Focus Publications

© 1994 David Jackman
ISBN 1-85792-066-X

Published by
Christian Focus Publications Ltd
Geanies House, Fearn, Ross-shire,
IV20 1TW, Scotland, Great Britain.

Cover design by Donna Macleod

Printed and bound in Great Britain by
Cox & Wyman Ltd, Reading, Berkshire.

Scripture quotations, unless otherwise indicated, are from
The New International Version,
published by Hodder and Stoughton

CONTENTS

1

Mind the Gap!

In a number of London underground stations, you will hear the same insistent message, repeated endlessly over the public address system, and even see it painted on the edge of the platform: 'Mind the gap!' As train after train pulls into a curving platform, and often at a steep pitch, the warning is very appropriate. There is a real danger, which is unexpected and could well be unnoticed. So it's worth the warning, before too many passengers put their best foot forward, into the void.

For very many people today, the teaching of Jesus of Nazareth is just such a void. The Bible is still the world's best seller. The person of Jesus is still the most admired figure in world history. But to the majority of our contemporaries, the Bible is a closed, unread bestseller and the person of Jesus an enigma, perceived at best only dimly, through the mists of time. Even those who claim to live by the Sermon on the Mount seem rarely to read it, and it is a remarkable fact of life that in many Christian churches the teaching of Jesus could almost be called forgotten, so little is it explained or applied. Mind the gap!

At first sight, it does seem an extraordinary paradox that a faith which is so clearly focused on a unique historical figure should pay so little serious attention to what he said. But we are two thousand years away, in a totally different cultural setting where our sense of the *now* has all but obliterated our memory of history and our quest for tomorrow consigns the lessons of yesterday to oblivion. It is not so difficult to see why the gap has occurred or why it continues to widen. The virtual collapse of the Sunday School movement, the decline of religious education in schools and the general hostility of the culture to anything traditional (of which the Christian faith is a major target) have combined to produce a generation of young people who have only the haziest ideas as to what Christianity believes or teaches. Even in terms of the basic Bible stories, which have run through our cultural heritage of the past five hundred years, we face a massive educational task, the dimensions of which have still to make an impact on most of us in the churches.

The gap of ignorance

Let me illustrate how the gap of ignorance exists, from an experience I had, some years ago, in talking to a student about the Christian message.

'Of course, I could never be a Christian,' he said, 'because I couldn't possibly accept the Old Testament.' So I thought this would be worth following up a little, and I said to him, 'What sort of things do you find difficult about the Old Testament?', thinking he might say the creation story in Genesis, but he didn't light on that. He said, 'Oh well, that stuff (as he called it) about Noah.' So I said, 'All right. What about Noah? What's the problem? You can't believe in a universal flood?' 'No,' he said, 'I've got no problem in believing that; I could believe in a universal flood. No, what I can't believe is the bit in the Bible where it says that when Noah came out of the ark, he picked up stones and threw them over his shoulder and they turned into people. That is the part that I cannot believe. That's why I couldn't be a Christian. I can't believe *that* sort of stuff.' I could hardly believe my good fortune! So I said to him, 'Shall we turn up the Bible, and see what it says?' Try as we might we could not find this great stumbling-block. I am not sure whose incredulity was greater when he turned to me and said, 'How extraordinary! I was sure somebody told me about it!'

He was not unintelligent; quite the opposite, in fact. But he had his number one reason why he should not bother to take Jesus Christ seriously, and it was tissue-thin ignorance. That young man was not unique. There are thousands of people all around us just like him. They have their reasons, often garbled and hardly thought through at all, but they have been sufficient to insulate them from ever taking the claims of Christ seriously, throughout their lives. It has been said rightly that when people stop believing in absolutes, because they have stopped believing in God, they do not believe in nothing; rather they are inclined to believe anything.

Believing the absurd

Evidence for the truth of this viewpoint is not hard to find. In the autumn of 1992, two books were published which reduced the Biblical picture of Jesus to absurdity. By reinterpreting what is called the 'surface' meaning of the New Testament Gospels (what Christians for generations have called the 'plain' meaning) according to criteria imposed from outside the Bible itself, it is possible through speculation and imaginative reconstruction to come up with a 'Jesus' radically different from that of the evangelists and apostles.

A. N. Wilson's portrait is of a first century Galilean holy man, one among many, a charismatic personality, a healer, but a Jesus of his time, whose teaching was nothing special. He was not born of a virgin and certainly was not raised from the dead. Indeed, there is no evidence he did anything supernatural.

Even more radically destructive is the Australian Barbara Thiering's treatment in *Jesus, the man*. On the strength of twenty years' study of the Dead Sea scrolls, she concludes that Jesus was an Essene leader at Qumran, a divorced man who was the father of three children, that he did not die on the cross, that he was in Rome in 64 A.D. and probably ended his days in the south of France.

At the same time (September 1992), *The Times* newspaper carried a report from the Council of Christians and Jews, in London, which claimed that Paul did not think of himself as a Christian at all, that it was unclear whether Jesus claimed to be the Messiah and that the Gospels have grossly distorted the teaching of the Pharisees. In fact, the Pharisees made a very creative contribution towards understanding God, and the Gospels were wrong to portray Jesus as hostile to the Pharisees. He was in fact very close to them in his teaching. Perhaps not surprisingly, the report is called *A New Look*.

What each of the examples has in common is a refusal to take the Jesus of the Gospels seriously. We may put that down to the secularisation of our culture, but that is only to ask a more fundamental question about the decline of Christian conviction and practical living in this century. If people all around us feel that the Christian faith is so trivial that it can be dismissed by these sorts of fanciful, speculative books and programmes, it may well be because they have never seen authentic Christianity being lived out in the lives of Christians. So

Peter Ackroyd in *The Times*, reviewing one of the books, writes, 'We can all believe what we wish.' That is very true to our contemporary culture, isn't it? 'Barbara Thiering,' he says, 'has performed a service in creating (notice the choice of verb, *creating*) an authentically powerful and partisan Christ to add to the existing images raised in his name.' What he is saying is that the Jesus of history cannot really be known. She has created this figure and he is only one Jesus among many others. There is a Marxist Jesus, a hippy Jesus, a social reformer Jesus, a philosopher Jesus. Now there is an Essene Galilean Jesus. 'There can be no sure knowledge in these matters,' he goes on, 'it is much better to retreat from fierce convictions into doubt and difficulty.' Mind the gap!

One of the Anglican bishops put it well a few years ago when he characterised the present religious climate in the West in the sentence, 'It doesn't matter what you believe, so long as you believe it doesn't matter.' But if that is the situation we have reached in our secular culture, it must be due largely to the unwillingness or inability of those within the historic churches to take Jesus seriously themselves. Why have we neglected and forgotten his penetrating teaching?

It was G. K. Chesterton who wrote that it was not that Christianity had been tried and found wanting, but that it had been found difficult and not tried. Certainly, to any student willing to do more than scratch the surface of Christ's teaching, what seems simple superficially is soon discovered to be profoundly stretching, and often hard to understand, or accept. The vivid immediacy and the concrete imagery of Jesus' teaching, rooted in a Middle Eastern culture so different from our own, do not respond easily to our more abstract thought patterns, or fit neatly into our systems and dogmatic structures which are characteristic of theological training. Because we often find it hard to fit the radical demands of Jesus into our comfortably worked out framework, we tend to leave them in revered isolation.

Scholars have their say

But perhaps the major reason why the churches have not taught the teaching of Jesus as much as they ought to, is because a great deal of New Testament academic scholarship in this century has succeeded in reducing levels of confidence in the teaching of Christ in the

Gospels. Tradition and redaction criticisms have had the effect of removing interest from the words of the Gospels and the actual teaching of Christ as recorded in them, to the shaping of the oral traditions by the first century church, or to the editing of their sources by the Gospel writers.

That is perfectly logical, of course. Once it is accepted that the sayings of Jesus, as recorded in the Gospels, were actually shaped over a period of time by the needs and life situations of the early church communities in which they were circulating, of course the interest will inevitably shift from the content to the question of authenticity and the criteria by which that can be established.

So, we have the critical criterion of 'multiple attestations', which means that only sayings which are repeated in independent traditions can be regarded as truly Christ's words. Another criterion is that of 'dissimilarity', which states that only a statement dissimilar from what Palestinian Judaism or early Christianity might have said can be ascribed with reasonable confidence to Jesus. But that, of course, makes the assumption that the teaching of Jesus never resembled contemporary Judaism (while both had their roots in the Old Testament) and that it was never adopted by the church. There is a real problem here for this theory. If the early Christians only passed on the tradition that fitted the life situation of their community, how can the criterion of authenticity be that of dissimilarity (i.e. traditions which did not reflect their life situation)? It is not my purpose here to try to refute the assertions of 20th century Gospel criticism, but to show that by substituting an interest in structure for meaning, and in authenticity rather than in application, academic scholarship has played its role in distancing the teaching of Jesus from both the contemporary preacher and his hearers.

One further way in which contemporary scholarship has affected our confidence in taking Jesus and his teaching seriously is in its assumption of a Greek or Aramaic origin of the Synoptic Gospels. This implies a potentially faulty transmission of the original words of Jesus in that they were being written down within a Greek-speaking church, a long way from the land and culture in which Jesus lived. It is also a long way from the famous second century statement attributed to Papias: 'Matthew put down the words of the Lord in the

Hebrew language and others have translated them, each as best he could.' It has been accepted as critical orthodoxy that Aramaic was the language of the people in first century Israel; to such an extent that the NIV has Paul speaking in Aramaic in Acts 21:10 and the heavenly voice at his conversion also speaking Aramaic in Acts 26:14, where in both cases Luke actually wrote 'the Hebrew language'. This is relegated to a footnote, as a possibility, by the translators.

But it is not a minor point. If we have to find an Aramaic original behind the Greek Gospels, which are then translated into English, it is not difficult to understand the frustration of the critics that they will ever be able to get back to the very words (ipsissima verba) of Jesus. If we cannot be sure of what he said, how can we take his teaching seriously? However, there is some fresh light in this dark, critical tunnel.

Research following the discovery of the Dead Sea scrolls has convinced a number of scholars in Israel that the commonly spoken and written language of the Jews in the first century was indeed Hebrew and that the Synoptic Gospels were in fact translated from original Hebrew sources. This is a view associated primarily with the work of Professor David Flusser of the Hebrew University of Jerusalem, a leading Jewish authority on the New Testament and the origins of Christianity. His case is that there are hundreds of examples of Semitic idioms in the Greek Gospels, which could only be Hebrew in origin. On the other hand, Flusser claims that there are none which could only be Aramaic, without also being good Hebrew.

From a different angle, this thesis is supported by Dr Robert Lindsay, a resident scholar in Jerusalem for the past forty years who with his research colleagues, David Bivin and Ray Bezzard, has written up his findings in a book called *Understanding the Difficult Words of Jesus*. They argue that sayings of Jesus which seem impossible to understand fully in English make excellent sense when they are translated back into Hebrew. The structure of the sentences, the literalisms and many of the idioms are all peculiarly Hebrew. Lindsay speaks of his attempt, in the 1950s, to translate the Greek text of Mark into a much needed modern Hebrew version. 'Rather to my surprise, the preliminary study of the Greek text of Mark turned up the conclusion that the Greek word order and idiom was more like Hebrew than literary Greek.' He tells how he felt himself to be restoring an original Hebrew work, rather than creating a new translation.

At the moment, these findings are perhaps only straws in the wind, but they could indicate a change in its direction, even for critical studies. As has so often been the case, the critical orthodoxy of the past may well prove to have been something of a diversion. The actual words of Jesus then become much more accessible than scholars have expected, and they are found to be rooted in Hebrew (and therefore Old Testament) vocabulary and thought forms. The Bible is then able to be seen once again as a unity, and its message demands that it should be understood and applied, rather than subjected to the slow death of a thousand qualifications. It is something to be worked and prayed for in our generation which so desperately needs to start taking Jesus seriously.

2

Identify the Key

Each book of the Bible has its own agenda and purpose. It was both inspired and preserved by the Holy Spirit to provide a particular revelation of the character and works of God, which none of the other 65 books does in quite the same way. There is both a unity and a differentiation between the books which make up God's self-revelation. So we can speak of the Bible as one book because behind the human authors is the one divine mind, inspiring, shaping and verbalising the truth. Yet the Holy Spirit's activity in inspiration does not over-ride or sublimate the individuality of the human authors, and they each write from their own particular point in history, along the line of progressive revelation, and with their own characteristic style and vocabulary.

Another way of making this point is to say that we need in our handling of Scripture the disciplines of both Systematic and Biblical theology.

Systematic theology gathers together material from the whole Bible, comparing Scripture with Scripture, in an attempt to formulate its unchanging truths in doctrinal statements, which encapsulate the revelation. Its weakness is likely to be an over-systematization, which forces individual texts into a preconceived framework, and which can do violence to the idiosyncratic nature of each single book. It can make the Bible overly abstract and drain it of its colour.

Biblical theology starts with the individual tree and attempts to understand the wood. It looks for the particular controlling principles of each author and seeks to understand the text in its own context before fitting the specific book into the big picture of God's revelation of salvation in history.

Both disciplines are needed. All of us inevitably operate from a doctrinal framework, which we need to check constantly against the meaning of any individual text we are studying. Similarly, every interpretation of an individual book, chapter or verse needs to be checked against the teaching of the rest of Scripture, on the ground that it cannot be contradictory of the plain meaning taught elsewhere. It is a constant dialogue between text and framework that deepens Biblical understanding.

In many New Testament books there is an interpretative key, which once discovered opens up the meaning and purpose of the writing in a wholly illuminating way. Perhaps the best known example comes from the end of John's Gospel (20:30-31):

> Jesus did many other miraculous signs in the presence of his disciples which are not recorded in this book. But these are written that you may believe that Jesus is the Christ, the Son of God, and that by believing you may have life in his name.

Here John presents us with a key by which we can understand the aim and shape of his book. In the epistles, the key is often contained in the opening verses of greeting, as in Titus 1:1:

> Paul, a servant of God and an apostle of Jesus Christ for the faith of God's elect and the knowledge of the truth that leads to godliness.

That is what this short pastoral letter is all about - truth leading to godly living. Sometimes, the same note occurs at the beginning and end of the book, as in Paul's magisterial letter to the Romans, where we are told in 1:5 his apostolic ministry is 'to call people from among all the Gentiles to this obedience that comes from faith'; and then at 16:26 that the gospel he has proclaimed and expounded is 'by the command of the Eternal God, so that all nations might believe and obey him'.

The genealogy of Jesus

But what about Matthew? Where can we find his key? The answer lies, of course, within the text of the Gospel itself, so we need to get to work on it. For a modern, western reader the start of the book could hardly be more unappetising. The first sixteen verses seem to us to be an almost endless list of names, which we cheerfully skip, to move on to the much more promising material of the birth narratives. Matthew, however, has a key purpose. In tracing the genealogy of Jesus from Abraham he establishes that he was a true Jew, and in taking his line through Judah to David, he is making a claim that the subject of the book stands in the royal line, perhaps even has a claim to the throne of David. We are alerted to claims about Jesus Christ being a true Israelite and being the Davidic king from the very start of the book.

This is a classic Biblical methodology. The genealogies represent real history, but they are presented in an individualistic Matthean way, as his careful structuring of this material into three sequences, each of fourteen names, makes clear. The historical events, together with the divinely given interpretation of them, constitutes the Biblical revelation. All through the Gospel this will be the case. The mighty deeds of Jesus explained by the gracious words of Jesus build our picture of him who is both Lord and Christ.

There is another important ingredient in the opening of the Gospel. Matthew is really saying that we can only understand the person who is the subject of his book, if we take into account all that has preceded him. Remove the page which the translators have inserted in our Bibles between the Old and New Testaments and the point is made. We shall constantly be referred back to the Old Testament part of the story of God's loving purposes for the human race, because that is the only way we shall find a key to understanding what Matthew will present to us as the climax of this process.

But it is equally true that only when we see what Christ has accomplished will some of the great mysteries of the Old Testament revelation start to come clear. It is a progressive revelation. We understand why Abraham left Ur, when we see the great redeemed community which Moses led up out of Egypt. We realize the importance of the exodus and conquest when we see David enthroned in Jerusalem, and the wealth and wisdom of the world coming to pay tribute to his son, Solomon. We see the horrors of the division of the kingdom and the exile in Babylon, but only understand their purpose when we hear the voice of John the Baptist calling in the desert, **'Prepare the way for the Lord, make straight paths for him'** (Matthew 3:3). It is only in this coming of the Christ that the exile is truly at an end.

Fulfilment of Old Testament prediction

All this helps to prepare us for the unmistakeable clarity with which Matthew presents his theme in the opening narrative passages of the Gospel, from 1:18 to 2:23. The evangelist who builds his book around five great teaching discourses here introduces five distinct narrative incidents. In 1:18-25, the circumstances surrounding the child's birth are given to his adoptive father Joseph, whose genealogy we have just traced. In 2:1-12, we see this infant born in David's royal line worshipped as king of the Jews by Gentile magi. In 2:13-15, Joseph is warned to flee to Egypt, with the child and his mother, from the wrath of Herod. The resulting massacre of the innocents is recorded in 2:16-18; while the fifth event, in 2:19-27, is the return of the family to Nazareth, following Herod's death. What binds the first passages together as a unit is not just their closeness in chronology (thirty years or so elapse before chapter 3), but that each story is presented as the key fulfilment of an Old Testament prophecy.

1:22 explains that Mary's child will be the Immanuel of Isaiah 7:14, 'God with us', born of a virgin. 2:6 identifies Bethlehem as the birth place of the king of the Jews, 'the shepherd of my people Israel', from Micah 5:2. The flight into Egypt is the fulfilment of Hosea 11:1, 'Out of Egypt I called my son' (2:15); while the massacre of baby boys in Bethlehem fulfils Jeremiah 31:15, where Rachel weeps in Ramah for her dead children (2:18). Finally, the return to Nazareth is attributed as the fulfilment of several prophecies. 2:23 tells us, **So was fulfilled what was said through the prophets: "He will be called a Nazarene."** References which may have been in Matthew's mind include Isaiah 9:1-2; 53:3, or perhaps Judges 13:5.

Modern interpreters are often startled, if not scandalized, by the way Matthew uses the Old Testament in these incidents. Is he just trying to provide 'proof texts', without any consideration of their original meaning or context? Some have suggested he is trying to score easy debating points against Jewish opponents of his Christian message. But the answer is much simpler. Matthew sees Jesus, as Jesus saw himself, to be the fulfilment of the Old Testament promises, and it is this key which opens up his book, as indeed it opens up the Old Testament itself. This is not to say that the interpretative principles which work on the grammatico-historical meaning of the text and are followed by conservative students of the Bible are to be jettisoned in favour of a more intuitive approach. Matthew was, after all, inspired in a way that you and I are not. In an article, published in the journal *Themelios* in the early 1980s, entitled *The Old Testament and Christian Faith*, Dr. John Goldingay makes the point very clearly. He writes:

> '... occasionally the form of words that a particular person uses may be so striking in some connection that the question of a second meaning in them arises. The way he (the Gospel writer) is able to identify this second meaning is his own faith in Jesus as the Christ. Matthew's interpretation of these passages from Old Testament prophecy, then, implies that when he looked back to the work of the prophets in the light of Christ, sometimes he found statements so appropriate to the circumstances of the Christ event that this reference must have been present in them from the beginning of God's will, if not in the awareness of their human authors.'

The Gospel presents, in a sense, a two-way conversation between itself and the Old Testament, in which we understand Christ in the light of Old Testament prophecy, but also that prophecy in the light of Christ, because he is its fulfilment. That is Matthew's key.

The next two chapters of the Gospel confirm and illustrate this further. As Jesus begins his public ministry, he claims to be the fulfilment of all that had been promised. But that inevitably brings him into confrontation and conflict with the existing historical Israel, the old covenant people. With the introduction of the adult Jesus, on the threshold of his ministry, in chapter 3, it is not surprising that John the Baptist's message is highlighted by Matthew, as a call to a baptism of repentance for the Jews.

That, of course, was normally something only required of Gentile proselytes; but John says to his Jewish hearers that they need to confess their sins and be baptised in the River Jordan. God is coming, he says, to raise up new children for Abraham (3:9-10) and the axe is already at the root of the tree. He is coming, to sift, to judge his people, to baptise with the Holy Spirit and with fire. As the wind of the Spirit blows, God will stand on his threshing-floor, winnowing fork in hand, to separate the wheat from the chaff, the true Israel from the false, and to burn up the latter with unquenchable fire (3:12). At the very beginning of Christ's ministry, through the forerunner's preaching, God is confronting the old Israel with the demands of their king.

It is highly significant that as Jesus is introduced (3:15), his first words, as teacher of God's truth and revealer of God's mind, concerning his baptism are, '**It is proper for us to do this to fulfil all righteousness.**' So, from the beginning, Jesus is introduced as the one who is pleasing to the Father, because he fulfils righteousness in a way that the nation, called as the firstborn out of Egypt (Exodus 4:22), has failed to do. His being pleasing to the Father is then authenticated by the descent of the Spirit, and by the verbal recognition from heaven of him as the beloved Son (verse 17): '**This is my Son whom I love; with him I am well pleased.**' Here is the righteous one who does the Father's will and with whom the Father is pleased.

Not surprisingly then, in chapter 4, we find Jesus, as the representative new Israel, facing the same temptations which the old Israel had faced in the wilderness, but coming through victoriously, where they had failed. In the temptation narrative, we see him being the true Israel, the fulfilment of Isaiah's prophecy that the people living in darkness will see a great light. Where Israel had failed to be the light to the nations which she was called to be, the king, who comes to declare his sovereign authority, is shown from the beginning to be the fulfilment of that prophecy (4:16). In Christ, the light has dawned. That is the meaning of his announcement of the kingdom with the next verse: **From that time on, Jesus began to preach, "Repent, for the kingdom of heaven is near"** (4:17). The disciples are called firstly to follow him and then, as a consequence, to become fishers of men, to bring others into the kingdom (4:18-22). The first unit of the Gospel narrative ends with the first members of the new Israel following the king, submitting to his kingly rule; and the true sons of Abraham following the Seed of Abraham, through whom 'all peoples on earth will be blessed' (Genesis 12:1-3; Galatians 3:16). Fulfilment is clearly the key.

In the introduction to his stimulating book *Matthew For Today*, Michael Green makes this penetrating point: 'Just as God has given the old covenant through Moses, so he gives the new covenant through the new Moses, Jesus, the one to whom Moses pointed forward.' He continues, 'Matthew is underlining the continuity of the new law with the old, the new leader with the old. Here is one greater than Moses giving to the people of God a new law, no longer externalised on tablets of stone, but written within their hearts.' This also explains the commitment to world evangelisation which has often been identified as a dominant characteristic of Matthew's Gospel. The book that begins with the Son of Abraham and David has no narrowly focused Jewish agenda. It ends with the king to whom all authority is given in heaven and on earth sending out his new covenant people to be the light-bearers to the nations as they go into all the world, baptising, teaching and discipling in fulfilment of the great commission (Matthew 28:18-20). This Gospel is designed to bring both Jew and Gentile into the fulfilment of the Messianic kingdom and to stress its continuity with and completion of all its Old Testament precedents in that kingly rule.

A key verse

With all these considerations in mind, we may well ask ourselves whether the Gospel contains a key verse, to sum up its message. Often in Old Testament narratives the key verse is found at the very heart or centre of the story and it could be argued that Matthew is working on this same characteristically Hebrew principle in constructing his Gospel. For me, the key verse comes as the climax of the first three teaching discourses and about half way through Matthew's story, as the confrontation of the new kingdom with the old Israel is beginning to move towards the ultimate rejection of the king. It is chapter 13, verse 52. After his disciples have affirmed that they do understand what Jesus has been teaching them regarding the kingdom, Jesus summarises his argument: **'Therefore every teacher of the law who has been instructed about the kingdom of heaven, is like the owner of a house who brings out of his storeroom new treasures as well as old.'**

Here is the continuity theme. The 'teacher of the law' is now 'instructed about the kingdom of heaven'. Those who have understood what God is saying in the Old Testament are being taught and instructed as to what the New Covenant is all about. Therefore from the storehouse of that revelation, like the owner of a house, they can bring out treasures which are new as well as old, because the new and old together form God's revelation.

Now it may well be, as some commentators have suggested, that the Gospel was primarily a tool for the Christian teacher. If so, we can see that Matthew has carefully ordered and packaged his material to teach who Jesus is and what it means to become his disciple. Certainly, it works very well for that purpose; it is a very strong Gospel from which to teach the gospel.

But 13:52 also helps to focus the confrontation theme, which runs alongside that of fulfilment. As the Messiah teaches, he confronts the old Israel with his claims to kingly authority over their lives. As he shows the new treasures, which are the long-awaited fulfilment of the old promises, he gathers to himself a new community of believers. His redefinition of the law takes them deeper into its original, penetrating demands; but his offer of mercy and grace also provides a way through forgiveness to freedom, and a new experience of the goodness of God. A new Israel is being formed from those who are willing to take Jesus seriously.

3

Use the Map

I am fascinated by maps. Holidaying in an area I don't know, the first thing I want to do is to buy the relevant Ordnance Survey Map, so as to begin to find my way around. It's amazing how much information can be packed on to one sheet. I guess it's a matter of temperament, and others may prefer the 'magical, mystery tour' approach, but I find my enjoyment of an area is enormously increased by some planning, based on careful map reading.

But, of course, it's all coded information. To someone who had never seen a map before, the very concept of a single sheet of paper representing a three-dimensional reality, thousands of times larger, would have to be grasped before the symbols could be recognised and translated. Moreover, this map has to be read accurately if we are to benefit by acting on its information. I like the story of the walking party, led by its map reader, who ploughed through bogs, waded through streams and clambered over barbed wire, all the time being assured that they were following the path on the map. Only at their lunch stop did they discover the inadequacy of their map reader, who had been following the county boundary!

In order to take Jesus seriously, we need a map. From the library of 66 books that constitutes the Bible, it is not unreasonable to select the four Gospels. From these, I have selected the Gospel of Matthew, simply because it provides us with the most detailed and ordered account of the teaching of Jesus. It is, in a very real sense, the teacher's Gospel. At the heart of it lies the concept that Jesus supremely reveals the will of God in his public teaching ministry, though what he says is often ignored and ultimately fiercely rejected. Nevertheless, in his words and in his mighty deeds which enact his teaching, Jesus is seen as the one who has come to reveal the mind and purposes of God. He is not solely a teacher; but teaching was his own priority and we shall not understand Matthew's purpose, much less

Christ's ministry, if we do not recognise the importance the spoken word plays as the core of the divine revelation.

Five teaching blocks

Matthew provides us with a map. His is a carefully constructed work, and he wants us to understand how it is put together, so that we can appreciate the priorities of Jesus which are inherent within this text. For example, nine of Matthew's twenty-eight chapters are given over to five major teaching sections, which create for us a predominant picture of Jesus as a rabbi, a truly great teacher who can interpret the mind of God. Jesus consciously gives himself this designation, as in the instructions he gives the disciples about the preparation of the Passover. **"Go into the city to a certain man and tell him, 'The teacher says: My appointed time is near ..."** (Matthew 26:18). It is significant too that he expressly forbids the disciples to call one another rabbi: **"for you have only one Master** (literally, *Teacher*) **and you are all brothers"** (Matthew 23:8). Jesus is clearly the teacher, par excellence and not even the apostles can compare with him. Not surprisingly, therefore, Matthew makes the teaching blocks the major feature of the landscape he is mapping.

We can isolate this material with confidence because of a famous formula, which concludes each of the teaching sections. This seems to be Matthew's own main structural division of the material in the Gospel. So for example, in chapter 7:28, we have the little key sentence: **When Jesus had finished saying these things, the crowds were amazed at his teaching.** That signals the end of a major unit, and it is not difficult to find where that unit begins in 5:1. Again we find the formula at 11:1: **After Jesus had finished instructing his twelve disciples, he went on from there to teach and preach in the towns of Galilee.** The third occasion it is used is chapter 13:53: **When Jesus had finished these parables he moved on from there.** Fourthly, we find it in chapter 19:1: **When Jesus had finished saying these things, he left Galilee and went into the region of Judea, to the other side of the Jordan.** Then, its last occurrence is in chapter 26:1: **When Jesus had finished saying all these things he said to his disciples, "As you know the Passover is two days away."** Clearly, that repeated use of the phrase is a marker post, a boundary line, which definitely and specifically draws a conclusion to a particular unit in the Gospel. So, the five units are:

chapters 5-7:	the Sermon on the Mount;
chapter 10:	the commissioning of the Twelve;
chapter 13:	the parables of the kingdom;
chapter 18:	the life of the kingdom community;
chapters 24-25:	the eschatological discourse just before Christ's betrayal.

These are the five major teaching sections in Matthew. We are not imposing them upon the text, because the author himself clearly maps out his material in this way.

Noting the large amount of Jewish material and the frequency of Old Testament quotations in Matthew, it is not surprising that commentators have drawn parallels between the five teaching discourses of the Gospel and the five books of Moses (Genesis to Deuteronomy) - the Torah. It seems to me to be labouring the point to try to find distinct mirror images between, say, Exodus and the commission to the disciples in Matthew 10 to proclaim the work of salvation. But it seems clear that Matthew intended to build his book on these five great statements of divine revelation, or teaching, because it is a new book of instruction for a new people of God. The message dictates the structure.

Further guidelines
There are, however, other evidences within the Gospel itself of careful organisation of the material. For example, the similarity of wording in 4:23 and 9:35 indicates a bracketing together of all the material in between, the two almost identical verses serving as bookends. At the beginning of the unit, Matthew provides us with a menu of what is to come: **Jesus went throughout Galilee, teaching in their synagogues, preaching the good news of the kingdom, and healing every disease and sickness among the people.** The early healing work in Galilee, the Sermon on the Mount, the healing of the leper, the centurion's servant, Peter's mother-in-law, the Gadarene demoniacs, the paralysed man and others, culminating in the raising

of the dead girl - all these are the fulfilment of that agenda. In broadest terms, chapters 5-7 are the preaching of the good news and chapters 8 and 9 the healing of every disease and sickness. Together, these two ingredients proclaim the king's identity and manifest the king's presence. So, 4:23-9:35 is shown to be a very carefully constructed unit.

But, there's more still to discover. For within what we have come to call the Sermon on the Mount, there are also features of the map which Matthew wants us to recognise and follow. The clue lies in the repeated verse at the beginning and the end. In 5:17, Jesus says, **'Do not think that I have come to abolish the Law or the Prophets; I have not come to abolish them but to fulfil them.'** The teaching section ends with a conscious echo of this verse at 7:12: **'this sums up the Law and the Prophets.'** Clearly the central teaching point of the 'Sermon' is contained within these two markers. It is signalling to us that this relationship of the new revelation to the old, the teaching of the king who has arrived as it relates to the law and the prophets, is the central body of content which the sermon is declaring. If we accept that there is a unit from 5:17 to 7:12, then we can look on 5:1-16 as the introduction, with the Beatitudes as the central definition of what membership of the kingdom signifies.

As we begin to understand Matthew's mapping techniques, it does not surprise us to find that the Beatitudes are also bracketed together, not only by the 'Blessed are ...' formula, but more significantly by the repeated statement at the beginning in 5:3 and at the end in 5:10, **'for theirs is the kingdom of heaven'**. Added to this, we can observe that these are the only verses where the blessedness is expressed in the present tense. Here is the *now* of the kingdom Jesus is inaugurating while all the other verses (4-9) express the *not yet* of the kingdom by means of the future tense ('they will ...').

So, we have the introduction that tells us what it means to be in the kingdom (5:1-16). Then the king's relationship to the old treasures, as he brings out the new treasures (5:17-7:12). And then finally, after 7:12, where he affirms, **'this sums up the Law and the Prophets,'** the application and appeal to action in 7:13-27. In the light of the king's arrival now, there is a narrow gate that must be entered, there is good fruit to be produced, the king's words must be heard and put into practice.

The dominant note is contrast. There are two gates, the two destinations, the good fruit and the evil fruit, obedience and disobedience, rock and sand, hearing and obeying, and hearing and refusing to obey. And in that sense there is a parallel to the end of the law code in Deuteronomy. We are to remember how Deuteronomy 30:19 says: 'I have set before you life and death, blessings and curses; now choose life that you may love the LORD your God, listen to his voice and hold fast to him. For the LORD is your life.' And it is as though with that in view, as Jesus comes to the end of this first great block of teaching, he similarly calls his hearers to choose life, to enter the narrow gate, to hear and obey his words, to build their house upon the rock.

We have time only at this stage to glimpse a little of the territory Matthew goes on to map out in his Gospel. We shall return to it in more detail as we follow through the great teaching passages. Chapter 10 brings us to an extension and development of the public teaching and healing ministry. In the first few verses, Jesus equips his disciples and sends them out to extend his ministry, and to challenge the whole of Galilee with his claims. The story inexorably moves on to the point where the king confronts his rebel people, ultimately in Jerusalem, their capital city, and, even more significantly, in the temple at the very heart of that city's life. And there he is finally rejected.

Leaving the temple, he pronounces judgment on unbelieving Israel. There, outside the camp, he is crucified and there he is vindicated by his resurrection from the dead. Significantly the last act of Matthew's drama is reserved for **Galilee of the Gentiles** (4:15) where, at the close of the Gospel, the sovereign Lord of life and death commissions his followers to a world-wide discipling ministry in every generation (28:18-20). He delegates to them his own unique authority, recognised at his birth by wise men (Gentiles) from the East and proved beyond doubt by his death and resurrection, to proclaim his kingship among the nations.

To see Matthew as the Gospel of the kingdom, the kingly rule of Christ, is very valid, since the theme clearly runs through both the narrative and the teaching sections of the book. The one worshipped as king of the Jews at his birth is eventually crucified as such by the sons of Abraham and the might of Rome. **'This is Jesus, the king of the Jews'** (27:37) has a deeper significance for Matthew than Pilate ever imagined, when he placed the written charge above his thorn-crowned head. It is a long journey from the early confrontation with Israel's spiritual complacency and externalism in the Galilean ministry, through the long section (chapters 11-20) where the story and the people themselves seem to oscillate between the twin poles of acceptance and rejection of the king, in his movement from Galilee to Jerusalem. Finally, chapters 21-28 show us the Messiah inaugurating the kingdom through the rejection of the cross and the vindication of the resurrection; confronting the very heart of the nation in David's city; and establishing, as a result of his atoning work, a new and universal Israel.

Matthew has provided us with the map. Now we must explore the territory.

4

Experience the Revolution

Chapters 5-7 of Matthew's Gospel comprise one of the most famous of all Christian instruction passages, which we have come to call the Sermon on the Mount. Immediately we face a problem, articulated by Graham Stanton, professor of New Testament at King's College, London. He writes, 'The sermon is well known to Christians today, but few appreciate the richness of these sayings of Jesus: their radical promises and demands have often been blurred, either through familiarity, or as a result of a precipitate quest for immediate relevance.' We are likely to face both dangers, as we study them for ourselves, or seek to teach them to others.

Now when he saw the crowds, Jesus went up on a mountainside and sat down. His disciples came to him and he began to teach them, saying:
    'Blessed are the poor in spirit,
        for theirs is the kingdom of heaven.
    Blessed are those who mourn,
        for they will be comforted.
    Blessed are the meek,
        for they will inherit the earth.
    Blessed are those who hunger and thirst for righteousness,
        for they will be filled.
    Blessed are the merciful,
        for they will be shown mercy.
    Blessed are the pure in heart,
        for they will see God.
    Blessed are the peacemakers,
        for they will be called sons of God.
    Blessed are those who are persecuted because of righteousness,
        for theirs is the kingdom of heaven.
    'Blessed are you when people insult you, persecute you and falsely say all kinds of evil against you because of me. Rejoice and be glad, because

Let's begin by noting the coherence of the three chapters. There seems to be no Biblical reason for doubting that we are dealing with the content of one prolonged teaching session. The introductory formula - **Now when he saw the crowds, he went up on a mountainside and sat down. His disciples came to him, and he began to teach them** - and the concluding formula, that the people had been listening in to many of these things and were amazed at his teaching when he had finished (7:28), are surely as inspired as the contents of the teaching. This is one consecutive unit.

But I think it is the unbiblical word *sermon* that often misleads us. Although the time taken to read the three chapters may be equivalent to the length of some modern sermons, it is transparently clear that what we have here is compressed, that Matthew is necessarily selective in what he records. Furthermore we are reading a translation of what was perhaps a Hebrew original. Certainly, we have a Greek version of something that was taught in another language, in a

---

great is your reward in heaven; for in the same way they persecuted the prophets who were before you.

'You are the salt of the earth. But if the salt loses its saltiness, how can it be made salty again? It is no longer good for anything, except to be thrown out and trampled by men.

'You are the light of the world. A city on a hill cannot be hidden. Neither do people light a lamp and put it under a bowl. Instead they put it on its stand, and it gives light to everyone in the house. In the same way, let your light shine before men, that they may see your good deeds and praise your Father in heaven.

'Do not think that I have come to abolish the Law or the Prophets; I have not come to abolish them, but to fulfil them. I tell you the truth, until heaven and earth disappear, not the smallest letter, not the least stroke of a pen, will by any means disappear from the Law, until everything is accomplished. Anyone who breaks one of the least of these commandments and teaches others to do the same will be called least in the kingdom of heaven, but whoever practises and teaches these commands will be called great in the kingdom of heaven. For I tell you that unless your righteousness surpasses that of the Pharisees and the teachers of the law, you will certainly not enter the kingdom of heaven' (Matthew 5:1-20).

compressed form. We know that the crowd sometimes spent days with Jesus and it seems likely that this material may well have been gathered out of one such teaching seminar, for which the disciples were the main target (5:1) but which many of the crowd were apparently able to overhear. We also need to remember that Jesus was a travelling preacher, that he would probably have preached the same material often, even repeatedly, and that the rabbinic method would be to present his material in an easily memorable form so that it could be learned by heart.

As we move the lens in to focus more closely on the detailed teaching of Jesus, we need to recognise that his overall purpose is twofold. Firstly, he will define the nature of the kingdom that is breaking in upon his hearers, and how they can become members of it. Secondly, he will relate the new treasure of the kingdom teaching to the old treasure of the law. Because we do not have the background of Old Testament thinking which was shared by all first century Jews, it will help us to look back to the pedigree of the kingdom idea in the Scriptures.

The kingdom has come

The Old Testament motif is of Yahweh, the LORD, as ruler and king, and of course it has a very long history which is everywhere assumed in Jesus' teaching. We can trace it back to the Exodus, where the chapters that precede the great deliverance chart the battle between the god-king Pharaoh and the mighty arm of the only God and king, Yahweh. He is Israel's sovereign; he is the one who delivers his people and constitutes the covenant community by his own mighty power. He rules Israel, not only by virtue of creation, but by virtue of redemption and by virtue of his covenant commitment to them. The kingship of Yahweh underlines this very relationship to his Old Testament people.

As the Old Testament proceeds, the later monarchy, for all its human limitations, is designed to be an expression of this. As Messianic expectation arose following the exile, and particularly in the inter-testamental period, the kingship of Yahweh increasingly focused on the desire for a transcendental, heavenly ruler to come. He would be the fulfilment of the picture in Daniel 7:13-14 of the Son of

Man who would come as universal judge, as Yahweh's ruler not only over the covenant community of Israel, but over all the earth. As Daniel describes it:

> He was given authority, glory and sovereign power: all peoples, nations and men of every language worshipped him. His dominion is an everlasting dominion, and his kingdom is one that will never be destroyed.

By the time of Jesus' birth, faithful sons of Abraham were looking for a Messiah to be king over Israel, to rule from Jerusalem over the whole world, to bring in an eternal kingdom to which every knee would bow, and which would never be destroyed. So, when he comes, what must he do? To them, the answer was obvious. He must defeat Israel's enemies, gather the scattered nation, restore Jerusalem, and rule the world from Zion. And when that happened, the just, that is Israel, would be rewarded, and the wicked, the nations, would be punished and put under his feet. The Davidic kingdom would be resurgent and political liberation would be secured. Increasingly, these hopes seem to have focused on direct, divine intervention. Expectations of miraculous deliverance were fed by apocalyptic writings, though there is some debate as to how much this was developed by Jesus' day. But, clearly, there was a growing agenda, which it was confidently expected Messiah would fulfil, when he came, at last.

In the narrower context of Matthew's Gospel, the theme is strongly present from the start of Jesus' adult life and ministry. We are prepared first for it by John the Baptist's preaching in the desert, **'Repent, for the kingdom of heaven is near'** (3:2). Literally 'the kingdom of the heavens', clearly synonymous with 'the kingdom of God' in the Synoptic Gospels, is upon us. It is bursting in on us, and the next chapter shows us why, as it introduces us to the arrival of the king. Following his baptism and temptation, Jesus takes on his lips exactly the same message, **'Repent, for the kingdom of heaven is near'** (4:17). The exact vocabulary has an interesting pedigree.

The Greek verb *engiken* might be better translated 'is about to appear'. It is used frequently in the Greek version of the Old Testament, the Septuagint, to translate a Hebrew verb (*karav*) which means 'to come up to and be alongside someone, to be with them'. For example, in 2 Kings 16:12, 'Ahaz approached the altar,' he came near to the altar, he got alongside it, he was there, and the verse goes on, he presented offerings on it. That's the basic meaning of the verb. And it is used idiomatically in Genesis 20:4: 'Abimelech had not gone near Sarah.' He had had no sexual relations with her. Also Isaiah 8:3: 'Isaiah came near to the prophetess, his wife, and she conceived.'

So if that is the Hebrew verb in the background, when Jesus comes saying the kingdom is near, he saying that it is present here and now, it is breaking in upon them at this moment. It makes sense because the king has arrived; he is here. It also helps us to understand that the New Testament concept of the kingdom is neither territorial, nor static; it is always dynamic, it is always active. It is the king's presence, as ruler, that constitutes his sovereignty, and those who are under his rule are the members of that kingdom.

Not unexpectedly, Matthew draws our attention to the evidence for the king's identity and authority in this long unit 4:23-9:35, supremely in his teaching and his miracles, which are the proof of the kingdom's reality. Indeed, Jesus makes this point in exactly the same way. In a parallel passage in Luke 11:20, he says, 'But if I drive out demons by the finger of God, then the kingdom of God has come to you.' It has arrived in the coming and revelation of the king. Similarly, the disciples are sent out in chapter 10 to preach and heal and cast out demons, because they are the demonstrable works and manifestations of the king and the kingdom. The towns and villages they visited were privileged to see God's power in action and were thereby challenged to acknowledge the king and submit to his rule. Already, by chapter 5, the ministry of Jesus has begun to produce this effect. He is at the height of his popularity. '**Large crowds from Galilee, the Decapolis** (the other side of the lake), **Jerusalem, Judea and the region across the Jordan followed him**' (4:25). With swarms of people drawn to him from all points of the compass, he now begins to explain to his disciples what it all means. He starts to teach them what it means to live under his kingly rule.

Subjects of the king

Blessed are the poor in spirit, for theirs is the kingdom of heaven (5:3).
I wish we could capture the significance of these words, as if we had never heard them before. Our problem, however, is not just over familiarity but the danger of profound misunderstanding. In our English translations, it sounds as though Jesus is laying down the entrance requirements for the kingdom: this is what you have to do to acquire your citizenship. The *blessing* Christ speaks of then becomes a sort of reward for gaining a righteousness which in terms of 5:20, '**surpasses that of the Pharisees and the teachers of the law**'. That is the way we tend to hear it.

And because our sinful hearts are so deceptive, and because as sinners we are inherently committed to works-religion, we always find it easier to interpret the gospel as law. We always want to turn the grace of the king into works. That is why the great British disease is to claim that we live up to the Sermon on the Mount. People say, 'I've never done anybody any harm; I live by the Sermon on the Mount!' But they don't, of course, because none of us can! When someone spoke to Martin Luther like that, his pithy reply made the point with characteristic penetration, 'We are not properly able to fulfil one tittle out of our own strength ... but must always crawl to Christ.'

That is one of the great purposes of the Sermon on the Mount; not to show us that here is a law which, if we fulfil, will bring us the kingdom of heaven as a reward, but that we cannot for one moment live up to this standard. We must 'crawl to Christ', because the great purpose of the Sermon is to show us that while we are not able to live like this, in the grace of God in the gospel, he makes provision for us to enjoy and experience it all. So when he says, '**Blessed are the poor in spirit for theirs is the kingdom of heaven**', Jesus is describing the kind of people who are members of the kingdom. It is not *theirs* in the sense that they possess it; it doesn't belong to them. But the mark of being a member of the kingdom is, firstly, that you know that you are a spiritual down-and-out; that as far as having anything to offer God is concerned, you and I are actually bankrupt before him.

That is 'blessedness'! The word *makarios* is actually the name given to the island of Cyprus, presumably because it was such a heaven on earth. It speaks of everything that is desirable. *Blessed* people are happy, most to be congratulated. In fact, in the Greek Old Testament, it is used to describe the experience of God's gift of salvation. Indeed, it is always related to salvation, so that Graham Stanton has suggested that we could accurately paraphrase the verse, 'God's gift of salvation is given to the poor in spirit' - those who are spiritual paupers. He admits that it would be clumsy to repeat this nine times in the Beatitudes, but it would give us a powerful understanding of what Jesus is really saying.

Here, then, is the definition of present membership of the kingdom. The kingdom of salvation has arrived, because the king has come. He is proclaiming his sovereign authority. All that the Old Testament promised is being fulfilled. As Dr Don Carson puts it in his commentary, 'The implicit commands of the Beatitudes are comprehensible only because of this new state of affairs.'[1] It is because of the gospel Jesus is proclaiming; because of the gifts of the king, the blessedness of his rule, that the characteristics of kingdom people are these which are outlined in the first half of each Beatitude. Jesus is saying that everything that the Old Testament pointed forward to, as that great hope and expectation, he is now fulfilling.

We can only rightly understand and interpret the Beatitudes when we relate them to their Old Testament origins, and recognise their fulfilment in Christ and his kingly rule. For example, in Isaiah 66:2, we read, 'This is the one I esteem: he who is humble and contrite in spirit, and trembles at my word.' Another translation could be 'spiritually poor and crippled'. The kingdom is made up of those who know that they have absolutely nothing to offer to God. He does not esteem those who, as it were, saunter into his presence, hands in pockets, confident that they must be accepted because of their moral record or religious devotion. It is the person who cries, 'God, have mercy on me, a sinner' who is accepted and justified (Luke 18: 13-14). Now that is the opposite of law. That is the antithesis of a spiritual meritocracy. God isn't interested in our merit - we have none. Jesus comes to us saying that if we are going to be members of his kingdom, we must take him seriously.

> Nothing in my hand I bring,
> Simply to your cross I cling.

Blessed are those who mourn, for they will be comforted (5:4).
Here, again, Christ is fulfilling the prophecy of Isaiah.

> 'The LORD has anointed me to preach good news to the poor ... to comfort all who mourn, and provide for those who grieve in Zion - to bestow on them a crown of beauty instead of ashes, the oil of gladness instead of mourning, and a garment of praise instead of a spirit of despair' (Isaiah 61: 1-3).

This, Jesus declares, is what his kingly rule is all about. Messianic blessings are beginning because the Rescuer has come, who will save his people from their sins. Therefore, those who mourn for their sins are the very ones whom he comforts. Those who claim to experience all the joys of the kingdom without any tears, don't understand its true nature. Entry to this kingdom is by mourning, by grieving that I am so unlike the king, by constantly confessing to him how far short I fall. God is not waiting for us to come and impress him - that's how we turn the gospel into law. No, Jesus says, take me seriously. When you are on your knees weeping about your sin, that is when you are blessed, that's when God comforts you, that's when you know his strength coming alongside to help.

Blessed are the meek, for they will inherit the earth (5:5).
As we look at the third Beatitude, we are taken back to Psalm 37, which is full of this idea.

> 'Those who hope in the LORD will inherit the land' (verse 9).
> 'The meek will inherit the land and enjoy great peace' (verse 11).
> 'The righteous will inherit the land and dwell in it for ever' (verse 29).
> 'Those the LORD blesses will inherit the land' (verse 22).

And Jesus says all that is being fulfilled in his arrival as king. All that the Old Testament foreshadowed in its motif of the Promised Land, the land flowing with milk and honey, a place of rest, will come to its climax in the new heavens and the new earth, where the dwelling-

place of God will ultimately be with men for ever and where righteousness will dwell. But it's all beginning to be fulfilled in the
blessings of the gospel. God's kingdom comes not to the strong and
the powerful, but to the meek, the gentle and the unpretentious. To
them is given the right to live with God forever. The right of abode in
the kingdom is the fruit of the new birth.

But do we really take Jesus that seriously? Don't we often find
ourselves thinking that God will not bless us because we haven't done
very well in our spiritual lives recently? There is a sort of controversy
between us and God. Somehow, we think that God is always out to
mark us down, always giving us hurdles to jump over that are just too
high, always knowing that we won't be able to succeed. But that is not
the way the Lord treats his people. He is a God of grace, who opens
his kingdom to the spiritually bankrupt, to those who know that they
have nothing to offer, to those who humble themselves under his
mighty hand.

So, when in verse 6 Jesus says, *Blessed are those who hunger
and thirst for righteousness, for they will be filled*, that appetite for
a right relation with God is able to be filled only in the kingly rule of
Jesus Christ. His kingdom opens the way into a personal heart
knowledge and relationship with God, which is deeply rewarding and
satisfying, because it is the very mode of life for which we were
created. No longer spoiled by our sin, or compromised by our partial
obedience, one day we shall be truly like him, for we shall see him as
he is. But even here and now, we experience, in our hunger and
thirsting for that, a measure of fulfilment. And one day fulfilment in
its totality, when we are in his presence.

It was John Wesley who recorded in his journal that he used often
to pray, 'Lord, cure me of my intermittent piety and make me thoroughly Christian.' That's hungering and thirsting for righteousness.
That's how you find spiritual satisfaction. One of the old Puritans
said, 'The secret of never thirsting is ever thirsting.' The more you
thirst the more you are satisfied. You see, it turns works-religion on
its head, doesn't it? It is only possible because of the kingly rule of
Christ and the indwelling power of his Spirit.

Blessed are the merciful, for they will be shown mercy (5:7).
Again there are echoes of the Old Testament in this verse. 'To the faithful you show yourself faithful ... to the pure you show yourself pure' (Psalm 18: 25-26). The reciprocal principle expressed there is a strong old covenant theme. If a man shuts his ears to the cries of the poor, he too will cry out and not be answered. But mercy is not a reward for good behaviour. Rather, it is a badge of membership of the kingdom, because those who know how great God's mercy has been to them, in providing entry, will demonstrate their gratitude in showing mercy to others. Again, Wesley records an encounter he had with a military general, who complained about the 'weakness' of the Christian message of free forgiveness. 'Mr. Wesley,' he said, 'I never forgive.' To which Wesley replied, 'Then sir, I hope you never sin.' When Christ came, his work was to bring the long-awaited mercy and forgiveness of God to a broken world, and the members of his kingdom are known for their likeness to the king.

Blessed are the pure in heart, for they will see God (5:8).
Cleanness at the very centre of our personal being (the heart) is a great gospel blessing. Indeed, in 15:19 Jesus identifies the heart as the source of all sin and defilement. To appear in God's presence, to see him as he is, requires total purity. 'Who may ascend the hill of the LORD? Who may stand in his holy place? He who has clean hands and a pure heart ...' (Psalm 24:3-4). It is to those who are pure in heart that God is good (Psalm 73:1). But what could never be ours by nature becomes ours through grace; and that grace, which cleanses our sinful hearts in this world, promises us the sight of God's glory in the next. Here, his people do see God in a measure, but it is at best 'a poor reflection as in a mirror' (1 Corinthians 13:12). The best of our earthly membership of the heavenly kingdom is summed up by Peter:

> Though you have not seen him, you love him; and even though you do not see him now, you believe in him and are filled with an inexpressible and glorious joy' (1 Peter 1:8).

So, although God has 'made his light shine in our hearts to give us the light of the knowledge of the glory of God in the face of Christ' (2 Corinthians 4:6) and we are being transformed into his likeness and do, in some measure, 'reflect the Lord's glory' (2 Corinthians 3:18), this is only a pale foreshadowing of what will be ours when we see God. The blessings of the kingdom are largely future in their fulfilment, though there are wonderful promises and down payments here, in this world.

Blessed are the peacemakers, for they will be called sons of God (5:9).

Children of God manifest the characteristics of their heavenly Father. We are only able to be members of the kingdom because the king has chosen to make peace through the blood of his cross, and so to reconcile rebels to himself. He is the 'God of peace', and the many Old Testament references to *shalom* all underline this. If then we are called his sons and daughters, we are also called to be peacemakers; not peace at any price, which is appeasement, but overcoming evil with good. The world may cynically, but truthfully, rewrite this sentence, 'Blessed are the peacemakers, for they shall be shot at by both sides.' That is the fallen world we live in. But the king who went to the cross to make our peace with God calls his followers to bear whatever suffering may come as we walk in his footsteps (1 Peter 2:20-23). And thinking like this prepares the way for the final Beatitude.

Blessed are those who are persecuted because of righteousness, for theirs is the kingdom of heaven (5:10).

We must not ignore the sudden jolt which this word is undoubtedly meant to administer. We would like to think we live in a world where good was rewarded and evil punished - provided that is, that our own sins were overlooked. But that is far from the reality. To be a member of the kingdom of heaven on earth is an amazing privilege. To know that I am spiritually bankrupt, to mourn for my sins, humbled under God's mighty hand, to hunger for righteousness, to show mercy to others, to be undivided in my heart's desire to see God and willing to be a peacemaker, when all that happens, will it not be heaven on earth? 'No,' says Jesus, 'it will mean persecution.' The whole world has been shocked by the horrors of so-called 'ethnic cleansing' in the former Yugoslavia, but Jesus is saying that there will be times when that sort of hatred will be let loose against the citizens of heaven by a sinful, rebellious world. Nevertheless, it is then, in the midst of all the problems, that the blessing of being the king's subject is truly experienced. We need to take his teaching seriously.

At verse 11, there is a sudden switch that brings the message right home to his hearers. Moving from generalizations about the nature of the kingdom in all places and at all times, Jesus changes to address the disciples directly, in the second person plural, 'Blessed are *you* ...'. They are not going to be immune from the implication of verse 10. Living as heavenly citizens in an alien world, they will be insulted, persecuted and falsely accused. Christians can expect all sorts of affliction and provocation, because of the Master they follow. Yet far from hiding away in a ghetto, or giving up in despair, they are to **Rejoice and be glad**. Is this some sort of unreal spiritual masochism? Far from it; this is the joy of a future reward, assured because enduring such persecution is the mark of spiritual authenticity (verse 12). It was always the mark of the faithful prophets in the Old Testament, and Jesus has come to bring that process to its ultimate fulfilment, as his later parable in 22:1-10 makes clear. So, his followers can expect that sort of rejection by the world.

Salt and light

But at the same time they will be its salt and light. That is why Jesus is not exhorting his disciples to try to be these things, but making a statement of fact, 'You are ...'. If we live under his kingly rule and exemplify the qualities of our Lord, then we will be salt penetrating the otherwise rotting meat of a fallen human society and light penetrating the darkness of human rebellion and rejection of God. Low profile anonymity will not be an option for Christ's followers, by virtue of the difference of their lives. Christians who are authentic disciples will always be like a city set on a hill, having high visibility.

Many of the commentators point out that these were pictures used in the Old Testament about the people of Israel. Just as the law that was given at Mount Sinai defined the name of Israel, so here, in a sense, is a new Torah, a new instruction, given to a new Israel. Quite often, in the teaching of the rabbis, Israel was referred to as salt, because they said they had a role to purify the nations by their separation from them and by their holiness. Also, in the Old Testament, the people of God are called the 'light', as in Isaiah where they are called to be light-bearers of God's revelation to the whole world (42:6; 49:6). Jesus takes these metaphors of penetration, and he says, 'That is the role I give to you, my people.'

It was a role that Israel had largely rejected throughout history. The story of Jonah is a classic representative example, where the prophet, like the nation, is unwilling to take God's word to the pagans and seems willing to go to almost any lengths to avoid the responsibility. But that will not be an option for the new covenant community. They will be like the new settlements you can see if you travel to Israel today, where little villages are springing up on top of the hills around Jerusalem. There is no way they could be hidden at all. Jesus is teaching us that light-bearing, evangelism we would call it, is central to the purpose of his kingdom. His people will stand out like hill-top villages, not because they self-consciously try to, but because of the sheer authenticity of their Christian living.

Sometimes this will produce a negative response: **persecuted because of righteousness** (verse 10); but not always, as verse 16 makes clear. Sometimes, it will produce a positive response - **your light [will] so shine before men, that they may see your good deeds and praise your Father in heaven**. But the predominant idea in what Jesus is saying is that this is the fulfilment, the continuity, the opening of the kingdom to the Gentile peoples. Here is what the Old Testament prophets said would happen, and it is all coming to fruition in the kingly rule of Jesus Christ. When once he enters the heart as sovereign Lord, there the kingdom of God is established. And just as he was able to say that he always did the things that please the Father, as the true Israel, the real Son, so all those who live under his kingly rule are grafted into Christ, the real vine, to produce that good fruit which brings glory to the heavenly Father.

Such priorities are extremely challenging for us personally, because they will not allow us to substitute outward religious conformity for inward spiritual reality, in our dealings either with God or our fellow human beings. The rest of the sermon is going to make that abundantly clear. It isn't by what I do, or how much I sacrifice; it isn't by my spiritual pedigree, or by the number of years I have been a member of a particular church, or an office-bearer in the congregation, that the reality of my Christian faith is to be measured. It is simply by how much I am submitting myself to the king's authority and casting myself, guilty, hungry and empty on his mercy and grace. Teaching like this is always highly confrontational to all forms of man-centred religion, which is why the Pharisees come increasingly into the picture at this point in the sermon, and why this growing conflict with the religious establishment of the day develops into such a major theme in Matthew.

Jesus is actually cutting right across all the values the Pharisees held most dear. The concept of being poor in spirit and mourning for sin is totally opposite to the picture of the Pharisee we are given in Luke 18:11-12: 'God, I thank you that I am not like other men – robbers, evildoers, adulterers – or even like this tax collector. I fast twice a week and give a tenth of all I get.' Or take the picture that we have in this very Gospel in chapter 23:5-7. They love the greetings in the marketplaces, the top seats in the synagogues and at the banquets, and people calling them rabbi. You see, Jesus' teaching is totally different. It cuts right into all that. This has already been heralded, in John's ministry in chapter 3, for the Pharisees are first introduced there in the Gospel, and when John saw many of them and the Sadducees coming, he said to them:

> 'You brood of vipers! Who warned you to flee from the coming wrath? Produce fruit in keeping with repentance. And do not think you can say to yourselves, "We have Abraham as our Father." I tell you that out of these stones God can raise up children for Abraham. The axe is already at the root of the trees, and every tree that does not produce good fruit will be cut down and thrown into the fire' (3:7-10).

We find it hard to regain the force of this, because from childhood many of us have been brought up to know that the Pharisees are the villains of the piece and should be booed whenever they appear on stage. But not in Jesus' day! As they send their high-powered delegation down from Jerusalem to examine this 'voice-in-the-desert', our first introduction to them in the Gospel is as a brood of vipers fleeing from the coming wrath. It is unlikely that they saw themselves in that role and even less likely that they would agree with John's verdict! They were the righteous ones, children of Abraham, the inheritors of the covenant promises. But John, as forerunner, requests some fruits of repentance as the proof, because if the tree does not produce good fruit God is going to chop it down. In fact, the axe is already out, sharpened and laid to the root. It will only take one blow for the tree to begin to fall. The message is truly shocking, but its imagery would be very familiar to the religious establishment in first century Israel. It is the Old Testament fulfilment theme that will bring it equally alive for us today.

In Isaiah 5:1-7 the prophet sings a song on behalf of God, about his vineyard. Set on a fertile hillside, the vineyard was dug, cleared of stones and planted with the choicest of vines. The owner built a watchtower, cut out a wine press and awaited a crop of fine grapes, only to be rewarded with foul fruit. The only remedy was destruction and that was what God called Isaiah to prophesy, for 'the vineyard of the Lord Almighty is the house of Israel, and the men of Judah are the garden of his delight.' The image of the vine is one which occurs elsewhere in the Old Testament as a symbol of God's covenant people and the loving care he had lavished upon them (see Psalm 80:8-19 or Ezekiel 15:1-8). It is still used as an emblem of the nation on contemporary Israeli coinage.

Isaiah's prophecy was partially fulfilled in the exile and the scattering of the nation, but the same divine requirements and disappointment are picked up and applied by John the Baptist to the Pharisees and Sadducees. God is going to cut down the tree. There has to be a new Israel. So, when we hear Jesus, in John 15:1, declare, 'I am the true, the real vine', that is what he is claiming. He fulfils all that the Old Testament people of God had failed to be, in his perfect obedience to the heavenly Father's will. As the branch out of Jesse's stump (Isaiah 11:1) he is the new vine, into which all his disciples are grafted, so that they may bear much fruit to God's glory, as the new Israel, the new covenant people.

The coming of the kingdom is therefore the establishment of that new community, under the authority of the sovereign Lord himself. As the kingdom is announced, God is serving notice on these religious leaders that this revolutionary kingdom is about to overwhelm their man-centred distortions about what God required, and to bring in a totally new order. However, the predominant idea is that of fulfilment and of continuity. The children are to reveal the family likeness, the Father's character. These men are not revealing a likeness to Abraham, let alone any likeness to God. Therefore, he will raise up new children of Abraham.

Christ and the law

We now come to a very important paragraph indeed, verses 17-20, which not only sets the tone for much of the rest of the sermon, but provides an essential foundation for understanding the whole of the rest of Christ's teaching in Matthew. The logical question, raised inevitably by what we have just been studying is, 'What then is the relationship of Christ to the Old Testament, and especially of his teaching to the Old Testament law?' Does this new teaching of the kingdom simplify the law of Moses, or reinterpret it, or perhaps even dismiss it? If he is a new Moses, creating a new Israel, where is there continuity and where a radical change? This issue broadens later in the New Testament into the whole discussion of the relationship between law and grace, so it is very basic.

The first thing that verse 17 unquestionably teaches is that there is a fundamental shift happening, in the coming of the kingdom, with regard to the role and importance of the Old Testament, summarised as the law and the prophets. In fact this comes out even more clearly a little later in Matthew's Gospel, in chapter 11:12-15:

> **From the days of John the Baptist until now, the kingdom of heaven has been forcefully advancing, and forceful men lay hold of it. For all the Prophets and the Law prophesied until John. And if you are willing to accept it, he is the Elijah who was to come. He who has ears, let him hear.**

A sea-change is happening. The prophets and the law were effective until John's coming, but from then until now the kingdom of heaven has been forcefully advancing. The parallel passage in Luke 16:16 is even clearer, where Jesus says, 'The Law and the Prophets were proclaimed until John. Since that time, the good news of the kingdom of God is being preached.' Clearly, the one replaces the other, but how?

Back in Matthew 5:17, the key word is *fulfil*. Christ has not come to *abolish* the law and the prophets, but to *fulfil*. In what sense? Matthew has already been providing us with the answer to that question in the earlier chapters. Jesus fulfils Hosea's prophecy (2:15) by completing its meaning. In his baptism, he fulfils all righteousness (3:15) by completing what God requires of him as he commences his ministry. Similarly, when he speaks of fulfilling the Old Testament he is talking about bringing all that it pointed towards to completion. What was anticipated is now coming to fruition. Jesus is not destroying the past, because the Old Testament is the expression of God's character and will, and as such is bound to be unchanging and eternal. He is completing it, not modifying it. He proved himself to be the true Son of God by doing the will of God from the heart, which is what he both requires and enables his new covenant people to do.

This helps us to understand verse 18 better. Every detail of the law remains valid until two things happen - this present world order passes away, and everything is accomplished, or all things come to pass. That probably means the completion of this great salvation plan of God for mankind that Christ has come to implement. All that the Old Testament spoke of will then be fulfilled, so that Christ's purpose in his coming is to move that forward through his life, death and resurrection to its ultimate triumph. It remains valid, but only in terms of Jesus' fulfilment of it. He is the one who fulfils the law and in his fulfilment of it alone, it remains valid for all time. This means that there is no option for us to try to fulfil the law in any other way than that in which Christ has already done it for us. We are saved, not by keeping God's law, but by receiving God's grace, made available to us through the only one who could keep, and then fulfil, that law. That is what closes the door to Pharisaism, as to all human-centred forms of works religion.

So, the fulfilment of the law for the kingdom community, in verse 19, is to submit to the teaching of Christ. He is the fulfilment of all that the Old Testament pointed forward to, and to live in the kingdom is therefore to be obedient to the king. The reference here must be to the Old Testament commandments, the instruction given in the Torah, the five books of Moses. **'Anyone who breaks one of the least of these commandments and teaches others to do the same will be called least in the kingdom of heaven, but whoever practises and teaches these commands will be called great in the kingdom of heaven.'** But they must be practised in the light of verses 17 and 18. If the law pointed forward to Christ and his teaching, then the proper way of living in the kingdom is to be obedient to the fulfilment of the law, that is, to the word of Jesus. That is why he tells us, at the end of the sermon, to hear and obey what he has said. The law was always designed to point to Christ, and it is only he who can show us how to relate to the law. But if we listen to him and obey him, we fulfil that law. Moreover, Jesus will show as the Gospel goes on, by the way in which he fulfils the Old Testament law, that the proper way to keep any of those commandments is to fulfil its purpose, not by detailed external rule-keeping, but by a heart of love for God, expressed in a child's obedience to please the Father.

I take that to be the point of verse 20, **For I tell you that unless your righteousness surpasses that of the Pharisees and the teachers of the law you will certainly not enter the kingdom of heaven.** It is hard for us to appreciate how that must have shocked his hearers, because the Pharisees devoted their lives to the law; they were its most stringent performers. The teachers of the law were the professionals; they expounded, developed and applied it to every conceivable situation of life. But in doing all this, they missed its true meaning and purpose, because their hearts were far from God, or from wanting to please the heavenly Father. As a result, they domesticated the law, and brought it down to their level. They hedged it around with so many qualifications and restrictions that in the end they even imagined that they could keep it. They became proud and self-sufficient, and so they kept themselves out of the kingdom. Because they made the law practicable for themselves, through their casuistry, they broke its ultimate, radical demands. Perhaps it is not so surprising that the Qumran community called the Pharisees 'seekers of smooth things'. They were the 'smoothies' of their day, concerned with outward compliance rather than heart-fulfilment. Their *image* meant everything to them.

Clearly there is a powerful message here for twentieth century Christians, if our righteousness is going to exceed theirs. Pharisaism is certainly alive and well, and living in some of the most correct, conservative and evangelical circles. Simply accepting the Christian, cultural norms around us, and living up to some sort of external standard of what that means, is to miss the whole purpose and direction of Christ's radical teaching. He hasn't come to destroy, but to fulfil the law and the prophets, and it is only in him, and through obedience to him, that our righteousness can be acceptable to God. Far from setting the Old Testament aside, Jesus brings it to its completion and teaches us that the mark of loyalty to him is that we are obedient to his teaching. Our king both teaches and lives the fulfilment of the law, by a genuine heart-love for the Father.

When we start to understand Christ's fulfilment of the law, we are immediately made aware of our own abject, spiritual poverty. When I measure my life by his standard, I see how far short I fall, and I recognise what the word of the gospel is, '**Blessed are the poor in spirit, for theirs is the kingdom of heaven.**' It is seeing myself alongside Christ, the fulfilment of the law, that drives me to recognise my spiritual bankruptcy, to mourn for my sin, to hunger and thirst for righteousness, and to seek God for mercy. That is the way into the kingdom. We become dependent entirely on grace.

This also explains why Christ does not destroy the law, and why this interpretation does not conflict with Paul's gospel of grace. The good news that it is only by grace that we can be justified, through faith in Jesus, is implicit within the declaration of Christ's kingly rule. In fact, the king's teaching immediately leads those who really hear his words to see the absolute necessity of grace. It drives us to him, in his gracious provision for our need. Far from contradicting the gospel of grace, Christ's teaching proclaims the very grounds of that gospel. Because he has fulfilled the law as our representative, he was able to die an atoning death in our place, so that we can be forgiven and justified. That is something the law could never do, but that is what it means to be a Christian.

It's that sort of Christian life that cuts into our culture, when people see us with a passion to become more like Christ. And that doesn't make us oddities but far more human than we have ever been before. The greatest contribution we can make to the evangelisation of this generation is our Christlikeness, our holiness, because where there is a holy church there will be a hungry world. Therefore, the world desperately needs to see Christian lives that are authentic. It needs to experience Christ's revolution. As someone said recently, 'What we urgently need is not more salesmen for Christianity; but more free samples.'

5

Catch the Contrast

In this chapter, we shall examine the application of the 'text', in which Jesus preaches the Sermon on the Mount, and then explore briefly the bridge that Matthew builds into the second great teaching passage of the Gospel, when the disciples are commissioned to spread Christ's teaching to the lost sheep of Israel, in the towns and villages of Galilee.

It is said that all the most powerful sermons teach one central idea, reinforced and applied with a variety of examples to a wide range of life-situations. Certainly, the Sermon on the Mount seems to conform to that pattern and there is no doubt as to what the central idea, the text, is. Stated in its most succinct form in 5:17, Jesus proclaimed, **'Do not think that I have come to abolish the Law or the Prophets; I have not come to abolish them but to fulfill them.'** As we have noted, it is an essential key to the teaching of Jesus, to the gospel and to the whole of the New Testament faith. John Bright makes the point very clearly:

> The New Testament rests on and is rooted in the Old. To ignore this fact is a serious error of method, and one that is bound to a fundamental misunderstanding of the Bible message. He who commits it has disregarded the central affirmation of the New Testament gospel itself, namely that Christ has come to make actual what the Old Testament hoped for, not to destroy it and replace it with a new and better faith.[2]

The heart of the matter

The rest of Matthew 5, verses 21-48, sets before us what the commentators have come to call 'the six antitheses'. That description is taken from the six contrasts, each one of which is central to the paragraph it governs. There are variations on the basic formula, but the core idea is expressed in both verses 21 and 33, **'You have heard that it** was said to the people long ago ...', and verses 22 and 34, 'But I tell you ...'. Unfortunately, the emphasis on contrast can obscure the main point, which is that of fulfilment. Perhaps to call them six examples of fulfilment would be preferable, for they are powerful illustrations of how the righteousness of Christ's disciples is to exceed that of the Pharisees and teachers of the law.

Here we have the foundation kingdom principles of 5:17-20 being worked through in a series of powerful, pertinent examples. Each one demonstrates the attitudes and behaviour which the king requires in those who submit to his sovereignty. Each one deepens the demands of the Old Testament law, by taking us to the heart of the matter, to its fulfilment in Christ. Our problem is that the unit is framed, at beginning and end, with what seem to us to be impossible requirements. They must have seemed impossible to the original disciples too: Your righteousness must exceed that of the Pharisees even to enter the kingdom (verse 20) and **Be perfect, therefore, as your heavenly Father is perfect** (verse 48). We have only to read the first paragraph (verses 21-26) to realise how completely impossible it seems:

> **You have heard that it was said to the people long ago, 'Do not murder, and anyone who murders will be subject to judgment.' But I tell you that anyone who is angry with his brother will be subject to judgment. Again, anyone who says to his brother, 'Raca,' is answerable to the Sanhedrin. But anyone who says, 'You fool!' will be in danger of the fire of hell.**
>
> **Therefore, if you are offering your gift at the altar and there remember that your brother has something against you, leave your gift there in front of the altar. First go and be reconciled to your brother; then come and offer your gift.**
>
> **Settle matters quickly with your adversary who is taking you to court. Do it while you are still with him on the way, or he may hand you over to the judge, and the judge may hand you over to the officer, and you may be thrown into prison. I tell you the truth, you will not get out until you have paid the last penny.**

How should we react to teaching like this? Many want to shrug it off as noble, but impossible, idealism. When you add the following stringent requirements, the lustful look being adultery in the heart, no divorce except for marital unfaithfulness, no taking of oaths, no resistance of an evil person, loving enemies and blessing those who curse us, it is not surprising that our reaction is 'You can't be serious!'

Some walk away from the teaching of Jesus as setting an unattainable standard. Some sink under its weight, aware of how far short of these demanding standards their lives are. Others, recognising this, determine to try all the harder to be good enough to pass Christ's searching examination and renew their efforts, beating themselves with the stick of the law to make themselves better Christians. Still others set about re-interpreting and domesticating what Christ said, so as to bring a diluted form of his teaching within the range of their accomplishment.

But nowhere in the three chapters of the sermon is there any reflection on our human inability to fulfil Christ's demands, but rather the astonishing fact that he expects his disciples to obey them. **'Therefore, everyone who hears these words of mine and puts them into practice is like a wise man who built his house on the rock'** (7:24). There seem to be no exception clauses here.

To understand what a proper response should be, we need to go back to the idea of the basic contrast built in to the six examples of fulfilment. In the first half of the formula, Jesus sometimes quotes the written law of God (Do not murder, Do not commit adultery) and sometimes adds the gloss of the teachers of the law, which was human instruction, without any divine sanction (Love your neighbour and hate your enemy, verse 43). In each case, this interpretation is minimalist. This was the righteousness of the Pharisees and teachers of the law. It involved external rule-keeping, without any real concern about the heart. The point is going to be made often by Jesus in his dialogues with the religious authorities, later in the Gospel. By adding their own exceptions and special cases to the plain meaning of the law they deprived it of its cutting-edge in their lives. Adding to God's word can destroy it as effectively as subtracting from it. So Jesus charges them, **'Thus you nullify the word of God for the sake of your tradition'** (15:6).

Again, he describes them as being **'like whitewashed tombs,** which look beautiful on the outside but on the inside are full of dead men's bones and everything unclean' (23:27). The Pharisees' 'righteousness' is just outward conformity to the standards of their peer group. It is not real righteousness in God's eyes at all, however orthodox and pious they might seem to everyone in their generation. Their wrong attitudes to God's law, exposed in chapter 5, inevitably lead to a false piety, in terms of the three great marks of their religion - almsgiving, prayer and fasting - revealed in 6:1-18. But there is a true righteousness, God's righteousness, which is sought by all who put the kingdom first in their priorities (6:33).

Just as it was the prerogative of the Old Testament king to declare his judgments, so Jesus, as the king from heaven, declares the true meaning of God's law, 'but I tell you'. But we must also remember how the sermon began. Disciples are those who have recognised their own spiritual bankruptcy before God and mourned over their sin. They are those who have received God's mercy and who hunger and thirst to be more like Jesus, living righteous and holy lives. Their aim is to live clean, devoted lives, at peace with God and bringing his peace to others. However, the key point is that they are not doing all this legalistically, that is, they are not trusting that these characteristics will make them acceptable to God. Rather they are living obediently, out of gratitude to God and drawing on the readily available resources of his grace to live lives that are distinctively different.

So, the point being made is that the law does not give life. It cannot. Entrance to, and membership of, the kingdom is not achieved by obedience to an external code, but by an inner conformity to the will of God that can only come about by submitting to the king, by hearing his words and putting them into practice. Unless we understand the demands which our Lord is making in this perspective of his grace, we shall turn the gospel into law and end up making the same mistakes as the Pharisees, either to our great self-satisfaction and pride, or, alternatively to our great despair.

Some commentators have suggested that the formula introduction used by Jesus is rabbinic. 'You have heard ...' meaning 'You have understood the meaning of the law to have been this,' 'But I say ...', meaning 'This is what it actually signifies, behind the literal understanding of the text.' Apparently, this was a structure which rabbis would use to give their particular interpretation of scripture, and if Jesus is following that, it would seem that he is saying, 'This is the way you have been thinking about it; I want to correct your thinking, so that you see that the ultimate meaning of that law intensifies its demand, because it internalises it.' He takes it from the outward behaviour to the motives of the heart, which is the true fulfilment of the law.

In this sense, the six examples all fulfil (or deepen) the law's demands. We have already quoted the first. Murder is deepened to anger. Of course, that is immediately a challenge to the law-keeping mentality, which wants to pride itself that the commandment has been kept, because the individual has never actually killed another person. Such a decent, respectable person would have no problem at all in identifying murder as the dreadful crime it is, whether in the first or the twentieth century. But surely that cannot be extended to anger? Everybody gets angry, don't they? Everybody calls their brother 'You fool!', at least at times of great exasperation. What can Jesus possibly mean? The answer seems to be precisely what he says. This is what fulfilling or 'filling full' the law is all about. Not only does he keep the law perfectly, but he also shows why its demands were made, and how deep its implications really are.

Thus, in verses 27-30, adultery is deepened to lust. In verses 31-32, divorce and Jesus' instruction about it goes beyond Old Testament teaching to the root of what marriage really is; that faithful covenant of friendship that was taught right from the beginning of Genesis. In the passage on oaths, the fourth fulfilment (verses 33-37), Jesus puts his own moral, radical demand alongside the common practice of using a lesser object for an oath, because it was thought then not to matter so much, so that you could break the oath more easily. He goes behind that to what an oath really signifies. In verses 38-42, the law governing retribution, he extends the Old Testament principle, which was designed to limit the taking of revenge, going much further than that, by seeing such events as occasions for love, rather than retaliation. Finally, in the last example (verses 43-48), on our attitude to enemies, Jesus again shows how he fills up the law by extending the demands to which the Pharisees had restricted it. The rabbis taught that hatred of your enemy was acceptable if it was accompanied by love for your neighbour, which in practice meant your fellow God-fearing Jew. By redefining 'neighbour' to include everyone, Jesus shows that you should not have enemies, because you cannot continue in enmity if you really love your fellow human being.

Here, then, we have the king declaring his judgments. He is not abrogating the *Torah*, but he is defining its demands at a much deeper level, through a much more profound and personal application. That is very threatening to formal orthodoxy, which is why, as soon as this teaching gets known, the Pharisaic opposition mounts incredibly. The natural tendency of the sinful heart of man is to be religious. If we think at all about ultimate values and realities, we will always go back to the idea of works-religion, of making ourselves right with whatever god we happen to believe in.

The Pharisees' legalism, which exalted the traditions of the forefathers above the deeper, personal heart-love for God, is the very thing Jesus deliberately challenges. It seems as though his teaching is specifically shaped that way; to expose the sin of Israel in its religious leaders, in the priorities which they had been happy to accept.

Of course, obedience is going to have its place in the kingdom. 'If you love me, keep my commandments,' he is going to say, but *his* commandments, not *ours*. So his confrontation with any sort of dry, legalistic externalism is very profound indeed. This teaching was never intended to be a code of ethics for society; it is the declaration of God's alternative society, what John Stott has called the 'Christian counter-culture'. It is directed to those who have already received forgiveness through the gospel, who live in the experience of Christ's kingly rule and who are therefore committed to working out their great salvation in gratitude, which issues in obedience.

Chapter 6 applies all this in the sphere of religious duty. The greater righteousness than the Pharisees, the perfection which the heavenly Father seeks, lies in the internal *purity of motive*. This is now worked out with regard to alms-giving, prayer and fasting, the three chief acts of Jewish piety. Jesus' case is that if these are merely to win men's approval, that is all they will win. But if they are done from the heart to please the Father, to fulfil all righteousness, then, while they will be as hidden as possible, they will also be rewarded openly.

For the **Father who sees what is done in secret, will reward you**
(6:4).

The emphasis of the sermon is constantly moving us away from
rules towards relationship. The greater righteousness is seen in purity
of motive, rather than outward observance. And having recognised
that pattern, we can then see why the so-called 'Golden Rule' at 7:12,
which ends the major teaching of the sermon is, in itself, a summary:
**In everything, do to others what you would have them do to you,
for this sums up the Law and the Prophets**. Here is this love in
action, expressed in its most positive form, which focuses the fulfilment of the Old Testament scriptures Christ came to bring in.

Response demanded

The epilogue to the sermon (7: 13-27) with its emphasis on the two
ways, the two destinations, the two kinds of fruit, and the two houses,
underlines and illustrates the two ways of responding to the Old
Testament revelation as Jesus is now proclaiming its fulfilment. In
fact, of course, the Old Testament itself often puts it in the same way.
Think of how Leviticus, Deuteronomy or Joshua end. They all call to
action on the basis of the choice that is being set before the hearer.

But here it is the word of Christ that is given that authoritative
status: **Therefore everyone who hears these words of mine and
puts them into practice**. He is putting himself, unequivocally, in the
position of law-giver, in the position of authoritative declarer of the
mind of God. This means that obedience to God is no longer simply
to study the Old Testament Torah and seek to practise it outwardly,
according to the traditions of men, but it is to hear and obey the words
of Jesus, out of love for the Father. This also explains why the context
of the sermon in Matthew is so significant. It is the good news of the
kingdom. The preacher, who has already been declared to be the king
in chapters 1 and 2, the Son of God in chapter 3, and the conqueror of
Satan in chapter 4, is now claiming to be the real Israel, the authoritative figure who directs the life of his people. The issue which the
Sermon presents is whether or not we accept the identity of the
preacher. Will we submit to his authority and obey his commands?
Will we recognise in him the fulfilment of the law and the prophets?
If we do take his message seriously, we shall recognise that apart from

his grace, we are never even able to approach the standards of righteousness that he requires, let alone fulfil them. It is indeed a preparation for the fuller exposition of the gospel, which unfolds as his teaching and his work develop.

No wonder that Matthew records the amazement of the crowds who had been listening in to this seminar on discipleship. It was like nothing they had ever heard before, not only in content, but in manner. We are also now in a position to appreciate more fully the cutting edge of the evangelist's account when he ends chapter 7 with the comment: **he taught as one who had authority, and not as their teachers of the law** (verse 29). We are never allowed to forget either the contrast, or the growing confrontation.

Earlier, we noted that the long section to 9:35 contained the two major ingredients of Jesus' ministry - teaching and healing - and following the sermon, the spotlight now falls on the second ingredient, in chapters 8 and 9. All the way through these two chapters, we see the fulfilment and confrontation themes being interwoven. On the one hand, this gospel is bearing fruit and growing. The healing of the centurion's servant in chapter 8 is an illustration of this fact. The covenant promise to Abraham, that in his seed all the nations of the earth will be blessed, is beginning to be fulfilled. Indeed, Jesus says of the centurion, **I have not found anyone in Israel with such great faith** (8:10). But with the fulfilment comes the confrontation: **I say to you that many will come from the east and the west, and will take their places at the feast with Abraham, Isaac and Jacob in the kingdom of heaven. But the subjects** (or sons) **of the kingdom will be thrown outside** (8:11-12).

No one in Israel is able to match up to the standard. We realise again how, by that comment, Jesus is sounding the death-knell of the old Israel. Think of the impact on that Jewish crowd when he says, **I have not found anyone in Israel with such great faith.** It is a major shifting of the goal-posts, because inward faith, not external characteristics, is now the membership requirement for the kingdom. That is why Gentiles will be admitted, people from the east and the west will come and take their places. And it is also why, even more shockingly, Jews will be excluded (verse 12) and the original subjects of the kingdom will be thrown outside.

The rabbis taught that to be a descendant of Abraham was the guarantee of eternal salvation and security, in and of itself. No orthodox Jew could ever be lost. But Jesus says that these are the ones who will be in the place of 'weeping and gnashing of teeth', precisely where the orthodox had always pictured the Gentiles would be. Clearly, the confrontation is going to be explosive. Jesus is claiming that faith in him, as demonstrated by the centurion, is the essence of that greater righteousness, and without that righteousness, there can be no residence in God's kingdom, irrespective of pedigree or apparent outward piety.

Yet, the Gentiles will reject him too. After he has healed the Gadarene demoniacs, **the whole town went out to meet Jesus. And when they saw him, they pleaded with him to leave their region** (8:34). It goes on happening all through chapter 9. In verse 8, following Jesus' healing of the paralytic, there is the recognition of his unique authority as God-given, by the crowd, **filled with awe.** In verse 33, **when the demon was driven out ..., The crowd was amazed and said, 'Nothing like this has ever been seen in Israel.'** The point Matthew is making is that this shows how far short of God's purposes the nation had actually fallen. If the powers of evil are not being routed among the people of God, what has gone wrong?

But with the fulfilment there also runs the confrontation. **At this, some of the teachers of the law said to themselves, "This fellow is blaspheming"** (verse 3). **When the Pharisees saw this, they asked his disciples, "Why does your teacher eat with the tax collectors and sinners?"** (verse 11). And most significantly, **But the Pharisees said, "It is by the prince of demons that he drives out demons"** (verse 34). The confrontation theme is also highlighted by the question of John's disciples in verse 14, as they come and ask, **'How is it that we and the Pharisees fast** (the old tradition, up to John), **but your disciples do not fast?'** By the end of the section the issue is clearly joined. Who is in the right? The traditionalists, or this young, untaught Galilean preacher?

The final verse, 9:34, presents a key summary of all that has been happening, in response to the teaching and the miracles. The insight and penetration of his words, coupled with the power and variety of his mighty deeds, are truly overwhelming. But after Jesus had made his unique claims and supported them in a way never seen before (or since), what is the considered opinion of the representatives of Israel's religious hierarchy concerning him? The answer is almost more staggering than the evidence itself: **It is by the prince of demons that he drives out demons**. That is how Matthew wants us to understand what is happening, at the end of this major section of the Gospel; and it makes the bridgehead to the next unit (9:36-11:1), of which chapter 10 is the second major teaching block of the Gospel. The three verses which introduce it (9:36-38) are, however, of great importance and merit our careful consideration.

> **When he saw the crowds, he had compassion on them, because they were harassed and helpless, like sheep without a shepherd. Then he said to his disciples, 'The harvest is plentiful but the workers are few. Ask the Lord of the harvest, therefore, to send out workers into his harvest field.'**

Once again, Matthew sets his story very clearly in its Old Testament context. In recording Jesus seeing the crowds, the old Israel, and having compassion on them because they were like shepherdless sheep, Matthew provides us with a powerful evocation of the teaching of Ezekiel, chapter 34.

There, God instructs his prophet to prophesy against the shepherds of Israel because they have used their office to take care of themselves rather than the flock of God. They eat the curds, clothe themselves with the wool and feast on the choice animals, but have no concern to strengthen the weak, heal the sick or bind up the injured. They do not search for the strays, but rule the flock harshly and brutally, so that the sheep are scattered and become a prey to the wild beasts. In effect, they have no shepherds. Therefore, God declares himself to be against the shepherds, who are responsible for his flock. He is going to remove them, and instead he promises, 'I myself will search for my sheep and look after them.'

Picking up this Old Testament motif, Matthew uses it to develop his fulfilment theme. The time is running out. The old shepherds of Israel have been served notice. The good shepherd has arrived, and he will create and shepherd a new flock. But because the task is so great he will send out his representatives to accomplish it, although they are all too few in number.

The metaphor changes to the harvest field, underlining the twin themes of opportunity and urgency, which begin to be interwoven, as Jesus explains to his disciples the nature and content of their mission, in chapter 10. The plentiful harvest underlines God's bounty, but the few labourers our human inadequacy. The answer lies with the Lord of the harvest, to whom all power belongs, but he wants to be asked to thrust out labourers into his field. Prayer provides the workers and prepares them for their otherwise insurmountable task of gathering the new people of God into the kingdom. It is to that role that the teaching of Jesus now turns.

6

Share the Vision

The second great teaching section of Matthew's Gospel is the instruction Jesus gives to his disciples (chapter 10), as they are about to be sent out on mission. Having told them that there is a great harvest to be reaped and that they are to pray for the sending out of labourers, Jesus calls the twelve disciples together and commissions them to begin to answer their own petitions. In many ways, it is a very exciting stage in the Gospel. He delegates to these comparatively raw recruits something of his own authority over disease and evil spirits. Expansion is on the agenda. The disciples are now to experience themselves being the channels by which God will do mighty works such as they have seen the Master do. The air is alive with the opportunity of sharing the good news of the kingdom with a much wider audience. You can almost feel the adrenalin flowing. But the strange thing is that the focus of the teaching of the chapter is on the opposition which the disciples will face: **I am sending you out like sheep among wolves. Therefore be shrewd as snakes, and as innocent as doves** (verse 16).

As they go on this mission task, they are going to face all sorts of problems. They will need great wisdom and they will need single-mindedness. They will need to be straightforward, committed, single-minded people; not gullible, not manipulators, not wheeler-dealers, but people who are guileless without being naive. R. T. France has a helpful sentence in his *Tyndale Commentary* where he says that Jesus did not envisage his people as a power group. Although he gives them his divine authority to go and fulfil the task, that pattern has already been set in chapter 5. Sometimes when you are working for the kingdom, you will be persecuted for righteousness' sake. Sometimes they will see your good works and glorify your Father who is in heaven. There will be both acceptance and rejection, as they go as Christ's ambassadors, in his name, identified with him

personally, the chosen representatives of their king. That comes out
very strongly at the end of the chapter in verse 40, the summary verse,
**He who receives you receives me, and he who receives me receives
the one who sent me.**

To receive the evangelist is to receive the message he brings, and
more than that, it is to receive the one whom the messenger represents.
For the message is to declare the kingship of Jesus, and the man who
is sent on the errand is invested with the same authority as if the king
himself came. That's the whole idea of being an ambassador, representing the sovereign. Jesus stands in the same relation to his Father
as the missionary disciples stand to him, in this context. Just as he
represents the Father, so they represent him. The missionary call of
the servant is parallel to the missionary obedience of the Son. So
anyone who receives a disciple, receives the one who sent Jesus. God
himself enters the house as Jesus' messengers are received. In the
confrontation that is bound to come as Christ fulfils the Old Testament promises and requirements, it will not be possible either to
separate Christ from the Father, or to separate Christ from his message. To reject his good news is ultimately to reject the king, and to
reject the king is to reject the Father, who sent him into the world.

With this big picture in place, we can now begin to examine some
of the specifics in Jesus' teaching about mission, which we also need
to take seriously. But we do need to be clear as to which ingredients
of the chapter are still applicable to us, and which were peculiar to the
twelve disciples at this particular point in history. This is in no way
to deny the authority or relevance of all that has been recorded for us
here; but we are clearly not forbidden to go to the Gentiles, nor are we
obliged to leave a change of clothing or our shoes at home when we
go on gospel business. All too often in our haste to make sure a Bible
passage speaks to us today, we fail to do the hard work of seeing what
it meant to its original recipients in a necessarily different cultural
context, so that we can rightly interpret its unchanging principles into
our own situation.

Temporary instructions
Clearly, the instruction to go only to the lost sheep of Israel is related
to a particular moment in history. This is the immediate focus of

Jesus' own work at this time, though as we have seen he responded to the Gentile centurion's faith even at this early stage. Matthew's interest is never exclusively Jewish, although it is not until the end of this book, following the completion of Christ's work in the cross and resurrection, and just before his ascension that he commissions his disciples to go into all the world and proclaim the good news to all the nations. That comes later, for very good reasons. Here, it is Israel that is especially in focus.

It was, of course, the same priority that moved the apostle Paul in his ministry, in which he saw himself as an apostle of the gospel, first for the Jew, then for the Gentile. If his own ministry became increasingly and specifically Gentile-focused, he never forgot that it was to the Jew first. But just as the Gospels end with Jesus leaving the temple and declaring that their house is left to Israel desolate, so the Acts of the Apostles ends in the same way, in chapter 28:23. Paul has arrived in Rome, and from morning till evening he explains and declares the kingdom of God, and tries to convince the Jews about Jesus from the law of Moses and the prophets.

The same emphases that we are seeing in Matthew ran right through the apostolic ministry. 'Some were convinced by what he said, but others would not believe. They disagreed among themselves and began to leave, after Paul had made this final statement: " The Holy Spirit spoke the truth to your ancestors when he said through Isaiah the prophet: 'Go to this people and say, You will ever be hearing but never be understanding; you will be ever seeing but never perceiving' " ' (Acts 28:25-26). Later we shall see Jesus taking up exactly that reference in Matthew 13, and there in Acts 28 Paul, quoting it concludes in verse 28, 'Therefore I want you to know that God's salvation has been sent to the Gentiles, and they will listen!'

Back in Matthew 10:7-8, we learn that their message of the coming of the kingdom would be authenticated by healing of the sick, raising of the dead and driving out demons. Again, there is a particularity to these instructions too. The truth of the message was confirmed by these wonders. Many claims are made for similar events happening today. There are missionary stories of extraordinary miracles, evidences of God's power, authenticating the proclamation of the good news in certain parts of the world where it has never penetrated before. We also know something of the Lord's intervention in healing the sick in answer to believing prayer, and of evil spirits being bound and driven out in the name of the Lord Jesus, in our contemporary world. There are even claims of present day resurrection though they always seem to be second or third hand and have not been satisfactorily confirmed. The twin dangers are that either we accept what often amount to fantasies, uncritically, or that we start to dictate to God what he can, or cannot, do.

The theological point, however, is that we have no need for such contemporary authentication of the gospel by the miraculous, because God has once for all confirmed its truth through the miracles of the Lord's earthly ministry and the apostolic church. Just as we are not to expect a personal encounter with the risen Lord such as Thomas had, where we see and handle his body, so we do not need miraculous evidences to continue to accompany gospel preaching. 'Blessed are those who have not seen and yet have believed' (John 20:29), Jesus told his disciples. We believe this testimony of the apostles who did see and hear the risen Lord, or we remain unbelievers. Similarly we believe the gospel on the grounds of its authentication by God's mighty works, as the New Testament records them, not because we see them today. The world may say that seeing is believing, but we believe because of what these apostles saw and did and recorded for us in the Bible. As John Woodhouse has pointed out, if the signs and wonders of the New Testament are insufficiently significant or wonderful for 20th century people, then we are not people of faith at all, but of rank unbelief.

The instructions in verses 9 and 10 also have a particularity restricted to these disciples at this time. They are not to be interpreted as a licence for any restless Christian to give up their job and launch out into 'serving the Lord', expecting other people to support them. When Jesus says, '**Do not take along any gold or silver or copper in your belts; take no bag for the journey, or extra tunic or sandals or a staff,**' it would have been foolish for his followers to interpret this as an all-time ban on carrying luggage! We are to remember that the message is primary and the messengers' life-style is to corroborate and illustrate it. They are to be totally dependent on God's providence. Venturing out on their Master's word, aware of his divine commission, they are to rely on him to be the means of which they are supported through the good will of those who will receive them. It is literally a journey of faith. **The worker is worth his keep** (verse 10) but it is because of the work (preaching the good news) that people open their houses to them. So, the messenger illustrates the faith and total commitment that lies at the heart of a true response to the message. It is that sort of exclusive self-giving that the king is always looking for in the members of his kingdom.

Always a realist, Jesus wants them to understand the rejection they will experience (verses 11-15). On arrival in a town or village, they are to search for a **worthy person**. This is nothing to do with status, resources, or even personal character, but much more someone who is able and willing, someone who will act on the message that is brought, by receiving the travellers, opening his home and contributing practical support. A 'worthy' person welcomes the messenger as he or she welcomes the king, just as a worthy disciple is one who puts everything at the king's disposal.

Opposition certain

Clearly, at verses 15-16 the immediate and particular instruction about this imminent mission ends, for at verse 17, Jesus begins to prepare his disciples for what will face them far beyond this first task. They are not yet being handed over to local councils and flogged in their synagogues, but the confrontation of the kingdom will make that inevitable; just as appearing before governors and kings, as witnesses, will be a future reality, only too familiar in the infant church. Jesus is setting the agenda for the Acts of the Apostles, and on beyond that for the centuries of persecution which the church has endured, and still endures, around the world. There is a progression in the chapter from the particular to the general, into the continuing experiences of the church in mission, being always **like sheep among wolves**.

This is where we 20th century Christians need to take Jesus seriously, especially in a culture that is tuned to hearing only the messages it chooses to listen to, and where the questions, 'Do I like it?', and 'Am I comfortable with it?' seem to screen out the question, 'Is it true?' Christians can expect to face hostility from an unbelieving world, however good the news is, because the message of Jesus Christ is a message of repentance, of a changed life, which makes moral demands on those who hear it, to put God first in their lives, rather than themselves. If we fail to do that in our own lives as Christian people, and if we do not take on board what Jesus is saying about the opposition that will inevitably arise as we share this message in the world, then we shall very soon give up spreading the gospel.

We shall opt for the 'low profile' Christian life, which is active and involved within our Christian fellowships, but almost invisible to the outside world. Lives like that rouse very little opposition from a secular society, especially when toleration is one of its greatest virtues. The world is quite happy for Christians to practise their faith in a privatized context, because that will not change the world. It was not until Martin Luther nailed his 95 theses to the door of the Castle Church in Wittenberg for all the world to read, that the revolutionary rediscovery of Biblical faith began to rock the medieval church and the political structures of European society. We can only choose to be 'incognito' Christians if we ignore Jesus' words about how desperate the needs of the lost world, all around us, really are. His kingdom is built by his rescue mission to lost people, among whom we are all included, from birth.

But 'gospelling' will always be hard work. We must not miss the impact of the timing of the warnings Jesus gives to these very inexperienced followers. The fact that the confrontation and rejection themes came so strongly, so early in their discipleship is indicative of how vitally important this strand of teaching was to the Lord Jesus. The inevitability of persecution is because of their message about the king. Notice how he says several times, it is because of me, **on my account** (verse 18), **All men will hate you because of me** (verse 22). There is solidarity between the king and the king's messengers. They are sent with the king's authority, in the king's name, to do the king's work, and where the servant suffers, the king suffers, and if the king is rejected, then the servant must expect to be rejected as well. So, when Saul of Tarsus is brought on his face in the dust before the risen Lord on the road to Damascus, Jesus says to him, 'I am Jesus whom you are persecuting' (Acts 9:5). Where the king is, there is the kingdom. Where the kingly rule of Jesus is seen in the hearts and lives of his obedient people, who take that message into the world, there the king will be rejected and hated, just as his servants will be the immediate objects of that rejection.

But that solidarity is also the ground of continuance. The identification with the king means not only that the servants will suffer, but that all the resources of the king will be available to them, as his representatives. As Christ's witnesses, his people can rely upon the fulfilment of the unique promise given in verses 19-20: **At that time you will be given what to say, for it will not be you speaking, but the Spirit of your Father speaking through you.** That is a unique expression in the New Testament. It indicates the distinctive relationship that already exists between those who are commissioned by the king to do his work and the Heavenly Father who has sent his Son into the world. If we identify with Christ in his ministry of gospel proclamation at whatever cost, God is identified with us in providing all the necessary resources to enable that mission to keep going forward.

The disciples needed that sort of assurance in the light of the terrible realities Jesus points to, as a result of their mission. In verse 21, it is family betrayal: **Brother will betray brother to death, and a father his child; children will rebel against their parents and have them put to death.** In verses 22-23, there is an implacable hatred that leads to persecution: **All men will hate you because of me. When you are persecuted in one place, flee to another.** Such statements may seem very remote from a comfortable Christian experience nearly 2,000 years later, but nothing has really changed. Bring the gospel to an ethnic community in the West and see young people respond to the claims of Christ and it will not be long before this sort of hatred surfaces, even within the family. In one community, whose pastor I know, a young woman was beaten up by her brother every Sunday for six months when she came back from church. In another family, when the father and brothers could not stop a young man from following Christ, they told him they would beat up his mother every time he went to a Christian meeting, and they did, so that he could not attend any longer. This is in a western, pluralist democracy, in the 1990s. The cost of following Jesus remains the same.

A student is not above his teacher, nor a servant above his master. It is enough for the student to be like his teacher, and the

servant like his master. If the head of the house has been called
Beelzebub, how much more the members of his household! (verses
24, 25). This is a very important principle of mission. Christianity is
not just a matter of listening to the teaching of Jesus and believing it
for oneself. It is a matter of living the teaching of Jesus and proclaiming it to others, wherever possible. In doing this, the messenger will
embody the message. For the message is about the king who has laid
aside his glory, to take on the humility of human flesh in the womb of
the virgin Mary; and who took that perfect life and allowed it to be
nailed to the cross, despising the shame, so that rebels might find
forgiveness, reconciliation and everlasting life. That is the kingdom
life-style which kingdom messengers are called upon to exemplify. It
can be very costly.

I believe that is why so much of this chapter is preparing the
disciples for the confrontation that they will inevitably face, as the
message of fulfilment bursts into the rotting fabric of Pharisaism.
And it is not surprising if there are ministers of the gospel today, who,
in trying to restore this gospel of fulfilment, the gospel of the kingdom, to churches that have degenerated into religious clubs, have
found the confrontation equally fierce and equally demanding. There
can be few more demanding ministry contexts than dry, legalistic,
outwardly orthodox churches, where the personal comfort of the
congregation has replaced any sort of obedience to the call to mission.
To bring into a congregation like that those rigorous demands from
the teaching of Jesus is to find that Pharisaism is alive and well. But
that is the test. If we are to model the message of our lifestyle it may
well mean that it is costly for us to acknowledge Christ before men, in
that context. Yet we must put him before anyone else, even when it
affects our homes, our families and relationships in our innermost
circle. It may well mean that we have a new sense of what it means to
take up our cross and die daily, if we are prepared to be truly
'gospelling' people.

Fear is the enemy
How, then, are Christ's people, whether in the first or any other
century to keep active in such a demanding, even threatening, task?
The rest of chapter 10 is devoted to some marvellously motivational

teaching on just that theme. From verse 26 onwards, Jesus shows the disciples and us three ways by which we could very easily be stopped from living authentic, Christian lives. They each contain a common thread, which is not difficult to spot. In verse 26 he says, '**Do not be afraid**,' and the phrase is repeated in verse 28 and again in verse 31. The continuance of his mission is threatened not so much by the persecution itself. The greater danger is that it will be neutralized from within by that great enemy, *fear*. On each occasion when Jesus tells his disciples not to be afraid, he gives them a perfectly good reason why they might well be. But with that realism there is given also the spiritual remedy in order to restore a true and total perspective on what is happening.

The first danger is *fear of slanderous accusations* (verses 25-27). Jesus has just referred to the fact that he is being called Beelzebub, the prince of demons. We have already heard from the Pharisees' lips, in 9:34, that Jesus is a tool of Beelzebub. But now Jesus tells us that they have gone further than that and identified him as the devil, in person. We need to stop and think what this would have meant to the disciples. The Pharisees were the religious authorities of their day. They were the people who set the tone, whose views really mattered. The disciples had been taught from childhood to revere the Pharisees, as holy men of God. So, when these men turn on the rabbi they have begun to follow and say that he is the devil himself, can we not feel something of the fear which must have gripped them? Have we really got it right? Are we really worshipping and serving the Lord? Is our view of Jesus the correct one? It is not just an intellectual question; their whole future depended on it, because it will not be so long before the servants are tarred with the same brush as their Master.

Our natural, human reaction to that sort of threat is fear, and theirs was no different. We don't particularly want to have to stand out against the tide. If people start to slander us because we are Christians, most of us would rather be carried along by the crowd, because that fear of man is in us all. Incidentally, that is also why the Pharisees were so opposed to Jesus. Their concern was to impress men; to be accepted for their ostentatious prayers on the street corners, for their obvious fasting, for their long robes, for their greetings in the market, and for their ritual washings. It was all outward show of religious performance. Everybody accepted it and looked up to it because it changed absolutely nothing. People will accept any sort of religious belief so long as it does not require any real change in their lives. But when Jesus came along, insisting on heart religion, their own fear of man would not allow the Pharisees to listen seriously to him, and so they determined to remove him. That's why he describes them later in this Gospel as 'blind guides and untrustworthy teachers'.

The great danger, then, is that this little band of disciples is going to be afraid of them. Then, they will start to compromise the truth. Jesus sums it up in verse 32-33: **Whoever acknowledges me before men, I will also acknowledge him before my Father in heaven. But whoever disowns me before men, I will disown him before my Father in heaven.** The temptation will be to give up under the pressure of slanderous accusations. Even in our day they can sometimes be very wild. Just before the collapse of communism in Eastern Europe, some Christians there were being accused by the atheistic authorities of being involved in child sacrifice. But for most of us the accusations are comparatively mild: 'Christians are all pretty inadequate people, aren't they? You may need a psychological crutch to get through life, but I don't. Surely you're not so out of touch as to believe the Bible, are you? Well, if you really want to be accepted here, then leave your Christianity at the door please. It's fine for you to have it at home or church, but don't start bringing it into the work place.' It is mild compared with what the apostles faced, yet we all know how such denigration can seal our lips. But Jesus says, '**Do not be afraid.**'

The reason is clearly given, in verse 26: **There is nothing concealed that will not be disclosed, or hidden that will not be made known.** Even in its immediate context, this has been proved so, by later history. When Jesus spoke these words nobody really knew what the Pharisees, chief priests and scribes were plotting. They imagined them to be godly men, who upheld the traditions of Israel and were closer to God than anyone else. But now the whole world knows the reality. Now it has been disclosed, and proclaimed from the house tops that they were actually not close to God at all. In spite of their outward religiosity, their hearts were far from him and hardened against him. Jesus is saying, to his first hearers and to us, that we need to take the long view, to live in the light of eternity rather than time, and with that comes the remedy for the fear of man, which is to go on proclaiming the truth.

So the Pharisees may be plotting behind Jesus' back, as indeed we know they were from the Gospels. They will do the same to the apostles later on. There may be all sorts of conspiracies and slanderous accusations against the church, but the church responds by proclaiming the gospel from the housetops. It is that message of truth, the whole truth and nothing but the truth, that everybody needs to hear. But to do that without fear, you need to have real confidence in the message. The truth of God's love in Christ is vindicated by people whose lives have been transformed by that love, and who are prepared to face these accusations, and still go on proclaiming the gospel openly. Do we take Jesus seriously on that? Do we trust him to sustain us in those situations? Do we believe that the answer to slander is to keep speaking the truth because it must prevail? We shall not see the turning of the tide in our society unless Christians start to have a renewed confidence in the power of the truth of the gospel to bring about a transformation.

The second threat is that of *physical persecution.* **Do not be afraid of those who kill the body but cannot kill the soul** (verse 28). Many of those listening to Jesus were actually going to die for their faith later on, as we now know, and Jesus says to them at this early stage, 'Yes, it may even come to that, to the ultimate sacrifice in acknowledging me.' And there are Christian brothers and sisters today, just a few hours away by air travel from where I am writing this book, who face just the same issue now.

Most of us contemporary Christians are afraid of being laughed at, or of being ignored by people we would like to take notice of us. But Jesus says, 'Don't be afraid even of those who kill you.' We are not to go back on our Christian testimony when we face tests like that, because they cannot do anything else to us. They may kill the body, but they cannot kill the soul. There is someone greater to fear (verse 28b) - **Rather be afraid of the One who can destroy both soul and body in hell**. As the paraphrase of Psalm 34:9 puts it, 'Fear him, ye saints, and you will have nothing else to fear.' The remedy for fear of man is a proper fear of God, and that requires us to take the long view, to judge by eternity, not time. To fear God is the only way to overcome the paralysing effects of human fear, which will otherwise stop us living authentic Christian lives.

But the third threat is perhaps the most powerful of all. It is what I would want to call the fear of *divine disinterest*. What if I do go out on a limb for God and he doesn't seem to come to my aid, or even to be hearing my prayers? When we get into difficult times and we find that our knees are knocking and our faith is feeble, we need to remember that Jesus said, **So don't be afraid; you are worth more than many sparrows** (verse 31). He has just told the disciples that although sparrows are two a penny among men, not one of them falls to the ground **apart from the will of your Father** (verse 29). It is an extraordinary saying. It is not just that God observes the sparrows fall; it cannot happen outside his will. If his care for the tiny and to us almost insignificant things of his creation is such, what will his Fatherly care be for his dearly loved children? If we are afraid that God will not care for the tiniest details of our lives, we have not yet learned to take him seriously. **And even the very hairs of your head are all numbered** (verse 30). Who could begin to do that? Some of us might have more chance of achieving a count than others, but until we get down to very small numbers, no-one would ever think of attempting it! In this vivid way Jesus assures us that God's ultimate knowledge points to his Fatherly concern.

Not only does he know us better than we could ever know ourselves, but he values and cares for us. As he sends us out as sheep in the midst of wolves, he does not leave us alone. He is with us, to protect and equip; he wants us to prove his faithfulness. Every one of his children is precious in his sight. The other side of the coin of fearing God is that the God we fear is our loving heavenly Father whom we trust and seek to obey. And if, as the hymn says, 'his love is as great as his power, and knows neither measure nor end,' then he will never lose interest in us. We meet the threats that the world may throw at us with the reality of the heavenly Father's love, as we have discovered it in the Lord Jesus Christ, and we take *him* seriously. It is not that God is so big that he cannot be bothered to care for us in that situation where he has placed us, with all those pressures and difficulties we are facing. It is that he is *so* big that he *can*!

When we come to him with our little problems or when, in the middle of the night, we wake up with those fears, and go round and round that circle of 'What if this?' and 'What if that?' how does God respond? As we bring it all to God in prayer, perhaps with very little faith, but saying, 'Oh Lord, please help me!', he does not say, 'Well, I'm sorry, you ought to have more faith in me; you've been a Christian a long time.' Nor do we get one of these messages when we come to pray to him: 'I'm sorry I can't answer your call at the moment, but if you would like to leave a message after the tone signal ...'. We are of much more value than many sparrows! He loves. He cares. He knows all about us. So we are to meet the threat with the reality of the Christ who has committed himself to us through his word and by his death on the cross.

The cost of being a follower of Christ

We come to the concluding part of this great discourse, from verse 34 onward, where we are encouraged to be realistic about the cost. **Do not suppose that I have come to bring peace to the earth. I did not come to bring peace, but a sword.** This is an important sentence because it confronts exactly what most of the Jews did think the Messiah would come to do, and what many of our contemporaries still think today. When Jesus was on the earth, the prevailing opinion amongst devout Jews was that the Messiah would expel the occupying Roman army, that he would lead the nation to victory and inaugurate a reign of peace and prosperity. There were plenty of Old Testament quotations that pointed to that - he was, after all, to be the Prince of Peace.

Today, many people would add New Testament quotations about 'peace on earth, goodwill to men'. Indeed, that is why so many assume that Christianity has failed. If Christianity has been around for nearly 2,000 years and there is still so much war, suffering and injustice in the world, as well as all the conflict between families and in personal lives, then surely Christ's claim to be the Prince of Peace is bogus. He's a failure.

The answer is always to look carefully at what Jesus says. He knew that this was just the mistake people were going to make, and he warns against it. The peace that Christ came to bring was peace with God through forgiveness of sins, and that was going to cost him his life. The only way a rebel world can be forgiven is by laying down its arms and surrendering to God's sovereignty, which is what we all, humanly speaking, naturally resist. So Jesus reminds us about the cost of being his followers, and he gives us a couple of examples where recognising him as Lord will bring a costly sacrifice into our Christian lives.

It may lead to *a family division* (verses 35-37). In following Christ, we are called upon to turn our backs on all rivals. Such a demand is neither unreasonable nor unusual. If you join up in the army, you turn your back on civilian life. If you sign a contract to become an employee of a firm, you cannot be employed by somebody else. If you get married, you say, 'Forsaking all others I will cleave to you as long as we both shall live.' It is not unreasonable. But what if our decision to follow Jesus and put him first is not ratified by those who are nearest and dearest to us? Then, says Jesus, there will be a sword of division in the family, even a man against his father, a daughter against her mother, and so on. He says, in fact, this is the result of his coming. Not that he came to destroy family relationships, far from it! But his coming into anyone's life inevitably separates them from those who do not respond to Christ's claims and acknowledge his lordship.

When it happens it is always very hard to take, but it is not a sign that everything has gone wrong. It may be the opposite, in fact. After all, when non-Christian parents see the children they have educated turning down bright career prospects, to go and bury themselves in a remote part of the world on some obscure piece of Christian service, it is not surprising that they cannot understand it and even cut them off. That is when the Christian, with heavy heart, has to apply verses 37-38: **Anyone who loves his father or mother more than me is not worthy of me; any one who loves his son or daughter more than me is not worthy of me**.

Far from being an invitation to destroy our family relationships, Jesus is saying that if the world is ever going to believe that this gospel is actually true, it has got to see that sort of quality, Christian commitment. We know how hard that is to put into practice, but we need to ask God's help to do it. It is one of the demands that Christ can rightly make of us because he is Lord. For if I put anyone else before Christ, then, practically, I deny his lordship in my life. I make an idol of a human being, however much I may love them and whoever they may be. In fact, we love them best by loving Christ more.

However, the watching world will assess the reality of our message not so much by our words as by our lives. Characteristically, Jesus is also more interested in the sort of people we are than in the work we do for him. The validity of the one depends on the other. Following Christ, then, will even involve taking up our own cross and losing our life for his sake (verses 38-39). Only such a disciple, Jesus says, is **worthy of me**.

In saying this, Jesus picks up a word of the Lord to Eli, from 1 Samuel 2:30, a verse that is often quoted out of context: 'Those who honour me I will honour, but those who despise me will be disdained.' Clearly that was behind what Christ is saying: '**Whoever acknowledges me before men, I will also acknowledge him before my Father in heaven. But whoever disowns me before men, I will disown him before my Father in heaven.**' It is very significant that this word of God to Eli came in a time of great moral and religious declension, and of widespread apostasy by the religious leaders of the nation. Here, in this context, it carries exactly the same sort of application. This declaration of the king makes fellowship with him the ground of acceptance with the Father. It is revolutionary: if you do not accept the Son, then the Father will not accept you. But if you acknowledge the Son, then the Father will acknowledge you.

Our problem is that we have romanticised the cross. People wear a cross on a chain around their neck. Inside and outside of church buildings crosses proliferate. It has become a familiar, anodyne symbol. But if you were carrying a cross in Jesus' day, it meant that you had no future, no control over your own circumstances, no way out. It was the mark of being in a cul-de-sac, with death at the end. To be unwilling to make that sort of commitment to Christ and the gospel is to disqualify myself from the name of disciple. It is to be a chocolate soldier rather than a true disciple.

Is that not immensely challenging to our late 20th century compromise-ridden evangelism? I want to be a follower of Jesus until he begins to cross my plans, or to challenge my prejudices, or until he begins to call me to do things that I don't want to do. But if I turn back at that point, how can I possibly claim to be a real disciple? No wonder the watching world will say, 'Oh, it's only religion. It's only an outward thing, there's nothing real to it. Don't bother with this gospel. It doesn't really work because when the going gets tough they give up.' What if it means not being accepted by the 'in' crowd, not being invited to the 'best' parties? What if it means not spending such a large proportion of your income on material things? What if it means not taking that promotion because if you did, you would have less time for God and his service, as well as less time for the family he has given you? That is real discipleship, living by God's priorities. Yet with every cross there is a resurrection, and every time we carry our cross for Christ we enter through it into a new experience of his power, not just to serve, but to be 'more than conquerors through him who loved us' (Romans 8:37).

Having looked realistically at the threats and the cost, Jesus ends his address by reminding his hearers of their enormous privilege. **Whoever loses his life for my sake will find it** (verse 39b). It is that little phrase, 'for my sake', which transforms our thinking. If we grasp at life in this world, what we can make of it or get from it, we are committing ourselves to disappointment. Ultimately, we leave and lose it all. But if we put Christ and his cause first, above our own desires and those of our nearest and dearest, we shall find eternal fulfilment. All the way through the chapter, this note has been sounding. It is vital for disciples to keep the eternal perspective clear. There is more at stake than present comforts or acceptance in this world. There is more at stake than present suffering. There is a far horizon; there is a long-term perspective. So in verse 15: **I tell you the truth, it will be more bearable for Sodom and Gomorrah on the day of judgment**. There is going to be a day of judgment. And in verse 23, the Son of Man is going to come, and when he does so the prophecy of Daniel 7:13-14 will be fulfilled, in his total authority and sovereign rule.

However, the chapter ends by Jesus underlining the privilege which already exists for his followers, here and now, in being identified with him (verses 40-42). If we go in Christ's name, to live for him day by day the authentic Christian life of dedication and commitment, we are identified with him, and he identifies with us. He gives to us his name, in which we go. Therefore, we do not need to be ashamed of this gospel, or to apologise for its message. We represent the king of kings, so that we can go anywhere in this world, and hold our heads up high, if we are carrying our cross and following him.

Moreover, we can be encouraged that the faithfulness which receives the messenger (verse 41) is rewarded just as surely and fully as being the messenger. To receive and act on God's word brings the same reward to the receiver as if he were a prophet himself. In fact, verse 42 expresses this principle in its extreme form: **And if anyone gives a cup of cold water to one of these little ones because he is my disciple, I tell you the truth, he will certainly not lose his reward**. The smallest courtesy in Israel was a cup of cold water; it was taken for granted. Anybody would give a cup of cold water if they had it, even to little ones, the least important people in their society. So, Jesus takes the least significant gift and the least significant people and he puts them together, to show that the God who controls the sparrow's fall and numbers the hairs of our head, knows and honours the slightest deed done for his glory. He is never in our debt. We can never outgive God. We need to take the privilege of investing our lives for Christ and his kingdom seriously.

That is the mission to which Jesus calls us and that is why every Christian believer counts. We may have differing gifts that suit us for different roles, but there is no hierarchy of importance in the kingdom. Each one is of more value than many sparrows. Each life has infinite potential with God. We can all build bridges into other people's lives, in order to share God's truth and love with others, who so desperately need it. There are people you can write to, people you can ring up, people you can speak to at the school gate, or the coffee break at work, people you travel next to on the train or the bus, or that neighbour who is shut in and never gets out and would love to have somebody visit. You can build bridges of friendship to people like that. It is whether we take Jesus seriously, or not. It is whether the gospel really is changing us, giving us love. You don't have to be great; you don't even have to be gifted though we are all more gifted than we recognise. You just have to be available! God wants to use you just as you are. That is the privilege of discipleship.

7

Understand the Issues

Chapter 13 of Matthew is the third great teaching discourse of the Gospel. Almost as well known as the Sermon on the Mount, it is the great collection of parables, which Jesus told the crowds. Until now his teaching has been addressed mainly to his followers, but at this mid-point in this story, we are given a comprehensive understanding of the message he brought to the multitudes. However, we are learning that Matthew, the theologian, orders and presents his material very carefully, to a set purpose. So, before we study the parables themselves it will be illuminating to set them in their Gospel context, by looking at the way chapters 11 and 12 form a bridge from the teaching on mission and prepare for what is to come.

Confrontation

We need always to keep the big picture in mind. Fulfilment and confrontation run hand in hand. Whenever Jesus claims to be the king whose sovereign rule is breaking into the old order of Judaism, he confronts the ingrained prejudices of tradition. Already we have heard the ominous note of rejection being sounded in the Gospel. That process gathers pace and intensifies in chapters 11 and 12. As Jesus teaches and preaches (instructs and proclaims) in the towns of Galilee (11:1) we discover developing opposition from the religious hierarchy, developing uncertainty among the people, but a developing understanding in the disciples.

In 11:2-6, we have a section about the doubts of John the Baptist. **'Are you the one who was to come, or should we expect someone else?'** In a sense, John's question articulates the debate that was raging throughout Galilee. Imprisoned by Herod, perhaps John recalled the promise of Isaiah that the Spirit-anointed Messiah would 'proclaim freedom for the captives and release from darkness for the prisoners' (Isaiah 61:1). That never came literally for John, who would soon lose his head, so was this why he questioned Christ's identity? Or was it that the judgment work he had proclaimed so powerfully in the desert seemed to be absent from the ministry of Jesus? In chapter 3:12, we learned that John had prophesied that the coming one would sweep away the old order and its corruption: **His winnowing fork is in his hand, and he will clear his threshing-floor, gathering his wheat into his barn and burning up the chaff with unquenchable fire.** But where is the fire? Where is the judgment? John probably sent his messengers to enquire about this.

In response, Jesus quotes extensively from Isaiah 35 and 61 to sum up his ministry to this point. The miracles attest that he is the expected one, and he is bringing in a new order. But significantly, what Jesus doesn't quote here are the lines from Isaiah about the day of God's vengeance and the day of judgment. What he says to John is that the miracles are demonstrating his identity, and the good news is being preached to the poor. The vengeance and judgment that are there in those Isaiah texts are not yet being worked out, because at this point the kingdom is here in blessing, not judgment. That will come as the parables of chapter 13 make abundantly clear, but at this point, it is a day of open doors and great opportunity.

Nevertheless, there is a current judgment on 'this generation', and as though to balance that point, 11:16 portrays Jesus likening it to dissatisfied, petulant children, sitting in the market place and protesting that when they wanted to play weddings their friends would not, and when they played the funeral dirge, they would not co-operate with that either. Nothing was ever right for such bad-tempered children, or for their cynical parents: **'For John came neither eating nor drinking, and they say, "He has a demon." The Son of Man came eating and drinking, and they say, "Here is a glutton and a drunkard, a friend of tax collectors and sinners"'** (verses 18-19).

Therefore, in verse 20, and following, Jesus denounces the communities in which many of his miracles had been performed. Although he has not yet swept away that old order, nevertheless in everything that happens, as the kingdom is being manifested, 'this generation' is being judged. Still, however, for the present time, it is a period of invitation and opportunity, so that the chapter ends with a great, universal call, **'Come to me, all you who are weary and**

burdened, and I will give you rest' (verse 28). In place of the yoke of the law, with all its additional Pharisaical requirements and additions, (the heavy load which they have placed on men's shoulders, 23:4), take the yoke of Christ and learn from him, learn from his teaching and from his gentle, humble example. This is the only way to soul-rest, because only in Christ's fulfilment of the law's demands can we have peace with God. Only in taking up his call to discipleship shall we discover the truth of his claim, **'For my yoke is easy and my burden is light'** (verse 30).

But if chapter 11 ends on this note of hope, chapter 12 confirms and renews the themes of confrontation and hostility. It contains the accounts of two controversies over the Sabbath, centred on the disciples' picking some ears of corn (verses 1-8) and on the healing of the man with a withered hand (verses 9-14). Both illustrate the heavy yoke of the Pharisees' legalism and how far from the underlying purpose of the law, and therefore from the heart of God, the religious experts had strayed. Though they claimed vigorously to keep every jot and tittle of the Old Testament law (with which Jesus agreed, 5:18), yet their behaviour actually demonstrated that they did not believe in its sufficiency.

Their additional requirements and exception clauses, the tradition of the elders, were in fact, an attempt to domesticate God's law, to bring it within range of their fulfilment by re-interpreting its demands. Instead of sitting under the law's authority, allowing it to convict them of their sinfulness, so that they could only come to God in abject humility, with a plea for mercy, the Pharisees avoided its impact at the level of the heart, refused to be humbled and instead allowed their diluted version of God's law to minister to their pride, in their ability to keep it. They had nullified the effect of the law, by taming it. And that is precisely what they were determined to do to Jesus, as well. They wanted to domesticate him, to avoid the rapier edge of his penetrating demands, to bring him down to their size.

That is what lies behind their demand in 12:38 for a miraculous sign from Jesus. Here is a head-on confrontation, as Jesus replies, **'A wicked and adulterous generation asks for a miraculous sign! But none will be given it except the sign of the prophet Jonah.'** The term *adulterous* here is being used in its Old Testament metaphorical sense of being unfaithful to the covenant made between God and his people. Adultery is frequently used by the prophets as a picture of idolatry, and we know that the Pharisees worshipped at the shrine of their own religiosity and imagined goodness (Matthew 6:2, 5, 16; cf. Luke 18: 9-14). To demand further miraculous evidences in the face of all that Jesus has been doing among them is simply proof of their determined unbelief; it is wickedly unfaithful to God's self-revelation. Verse 40 explains that the sign of Jonah in the resurrection will be the incontrovertible evidence of the deity of Christ.

But verses 41-42 take the fulfilment theme on further, as Jesus claims to be greater than Jonah and greater than Solomon. The point is that Nineveh, a pagan city, repented at Jonah's preaching, and the Queen of Sheba, a pagan monarch, acknowledged the supremacy of the living God, through Solomon's wisdom. But the adulterous leaders of Israel will not respond to the preaching of one who is greater than Jonah and wiser than Solomon. They have so hardened their hearts, that they are determined not to believe, whatever the evidence.

So, Jesus says, they are like a man who, having been delivered from an evil spirit, is invaded by seven other more wicked spirits and is in a far worse state than at the beginning, because there was a vacuum in the man's life that was not filled by God (verses 43-45). Neutrality on the issues which Jesus was raising was an impossibility, whether it was the keeping of the law or the identity of the teacher. They had been confronted with divine power, which they could not simply shrug off. Jesus is moving them towards the crisis. As Leon Morris puts it, 'If it continued on its self-opinionated way, the generation that refused the opportunity presented to it by the appearance in its midst of the very Son of God, the generation already characterised as "evil and adulterous", faced a future that was bleak indeed.' Already chapter 12 has shown us that they are plotting to kill Jesus (verse 14), which shows what they really thought of the ten commandments, and they are publicly attributing his mighty works to the devil (verse 24). To call God evil and to harden one's heart against God's truth by calling it a lie is the blasphemy against the Holy Spirit, of which Jesus warns them in verses 30-32. It is because of their rank unbelief and deliberate unfaithfulness that their house is over-run by evil powers and is about to fall under the judgment of the king.

The great danger for us is encapsulated in the story of the Sunday School teacher who, after teaching the parable of the Pharisee and the tax-collector from Luke 18, ended his lesson, 'Now, boys and girls, let's just thank God that we are not like the Pharisee.' It is all too easy to do. We can distance ourselves from what is to us their obvious hypocrisy without detecting its roots in our own hearts. Do we not often want to domesticate Jesus? We want him to dance to our tune and produce miraculous answers to our prayers. We reduce him to a divine slot-machine whom we can manipulate and over whom we have control, because we use the right formulae or perform the right actions.

Contemporary Pharisaism is well illustrated by a poster I saw outside a church at New Year, three years ago. It read, 'Trust a great God to help you fulfil your potential.' The first few words are certainly right, but that is all! Certainly, he is a great God and we should trust him, but do we really think the world revolves around us and our pathetic *potential* rather than around his sovereign majesty and divine will? It is very typical of the 1990s to think that way, to imagine that God exists to meet my needs, and it is the heart of Pharisaism. 'You can buy our support,' they say in effect to Jesus, 'provided you give us the right signs, provided you dance to our tune.' As soon as we begin to put ourselves at the centre of the universe and imagine that God somehow exists to meet our felt needs, we reveal what sons of Adam and daughters of Eve we really are. Whatever our religious profession may be, we have actually joined our faithless generation which is always dedicated to bringing God down to our human level, and always finding reasons not to respond to his word, for not taking Jesus seriously.

In God's kingdom, however, believing is not on the basis of miraculous signs, but on the basis of the Son of Man's death and resurrection (verse 40). The chapter ends with a powerful definition of what the new Israel, the new faithful covenant community, is to be. When the mother and brothers of Jesus come to speak to him, he uses the opportunity to redefine what it means to be related to God as a member of his family. It has nothing to do with human descent, as the physical sons of Abraham love to claim. '**For whoever does the will of my Father in heaven is my brother and sister and mother**' (verse 50). Nothing about bir:h; everything about obedience. We have seen it already in 7:21, 'Not everyone who says to me, "Lord, Lord," will enter the kingdom of heaven, but only he who does the will of my Father who is in heaven.' In this twelfth chapter, Jesus has also reiterated the idea of the fruitless tree that is only fit to be chopped down (cf. 3:10, 7:17-20): 'Make a tree good and its fruit will be good, or make a tree bad and its fruit will be bad, for a tree is recognised by its fruit' (verse 33). The new community is being created. The declaration of the kingdom is gathering its members, but they are only those who hear and do what the king commands.

Why parables?

With this context background clearly in our minds, we are now in a position to understand and appreciate the great chapter of parables more fully. But what are the parables of Jesus doing? Many of us were taught in childhood that a parable is 'an earthly story with a heavenly meaning'. Scholars have claimed that each story is designed to teach one main lesson, which is a valuable corrective against allegorisation of all the details, but may not be the whole story. In some parables, different ingredients do have symbolic significance, as with the different soils in the parable of the sower.

But we are surely right to run from the allegorising method beloved of the medieval church, where, in the parable of the Good Samaritan, for example, the two pence stands for the sacraments of baptism and holy communion, and the inn becomes the church where the traveller waits for the Lord's return. The problem with all such interpretation is not its ingenuity but that it is arbitrary. It is imposed on the text, rather than read out from it, so that it carries no greater authority than that of their interpreter's intellect (or imagination!).

Some describe the parables as works of art; others as 'weapons of conflict', in the sense that they are subversive, they get under the skin, and begin to make the truth bite. Jesus uses unusual examples. Here, in chapter 13, the yeast in the dough, usually a picture in Jewish thought of the penetration of evil, is actually a picture of the penetration of the kingdom. Parables make you stop and think; they demand interpretation. They point to other realities. They are not merely stories to enjoy; they hold up one reality to serve as a mirror of another, the kingdom of God. They are avenues to understanding, handles by which we can grasp the meaning of the kingdom.

We have already had some indication of how Jesus can do that in a one verse parable in 12:29: '**... how can anyone enter a strong man's home and carry off his possessions unless he first ties up the strong man? Then he can rob his house.**' That is a strong statement about the presence of the kingdom in response to the Pharisees' accusation that Jesus is working by the power of the devil. Jesus affirms that his power is stronger than Satan's, that he is in fact plundering the devil's goods. That is what the breaking in of the kingdom of heaven achieves. Of course, if we use the verse to try to discuss the ethics of whether we should bind up strong men and rob their houses, we entirely miss the point. Jesus is painting a vivid little picture that helps us understand the spiritual reality of what is going on through his ministry. It helps us grasp what he is actually doing. Similarly, in chapter 13, we have seven parables gathered together, in order to clarify and deepen our understanding as to what the penetration of the kingdom of heaven on earth is really all about.

The first and largest section is devoted to the parable of the Sower, or, as we should call it, the parable of the Soils, and then there follow six others. Three of them are told to the crowds, **Jesus spoke all these things to the crowd in parables** (verse 34), and those three are the parables of the Wheat and the Weeds (verses 24-30), the Mustard Seed (verses 31-32) and the Yeast in the Dough (verse 33). The remaining three are told to the disciples (verse 36). They are the parables of the Treasure in the Field (verse 44), the Priceless Pearl (verses 45-46) and the Dragnet (verses 47-50). In this section, we also have the authoritative interpretation by Jesus of the Wheat and the Weeds, in verses 36-43.

Now clearly the first and last of the six are similar: the Wheat and the Weeds and the Dragnet are both parables about the sifting at the end of the age, the discrimination that is the act of God's final judgment. Parables 2 and 3 also belong together. They are both told to the crowd. They follow one another and they are both parables, in the broadest sense, about the growth of the kingdom. Similarly, 4 and 5, the Buried Treasure and the Priceless Pearl, belong together. They are told to the disciples and they are all about the value of the kingdom.

That is one way of looking at the material, and helping us to understand how it has been ordered.

However, another way, which I think blends in with that, is to see this as a chapter which has gathered the parables together, because they are all answering important questions which have been thrown up by the fulfilment and confrontation themes in the first twelve chapters of the Gospel. At this mid-point in the Gospel, we are, as it were, taking a breather, to sort out what Jesus has been saying about the kingdom, and what the kingdom realities really are. I have found it helpful to follow the suggestion that there are at least three major questions being answered by these parables.

The first is, *If the kingdom of heaven is really here, in the ministry of Jesus, why is the response so varied, or even muted?* There are multitudes of people interested in his healing miracles - who would not be in days when medical science hardly existed? But it is not apparent that many are becoming committed disciples. The question must have been on everyone's lips, 'Is this the Son of David?' (12:23). 'Is this the one who was to come, the Messiah?' (11:3). If so, why does it all seem so unsuccessful? The Romans are still in control of the country. An extension of this question is to ask, *How can the kingdom be here when evil is obviously so continuously present?* If the Christ has come to right wrongs then why has he not done it, on the grand scale?

The second problem addressed is, *How can the kingdom be here, if it seems to be spreading so little, or so slowly? Why is its impact so limited?* Most orthodox Jews seem to have expected that when the Messiah came, it would be with unmistakable power. He would claim the throne of David in Jerusalem, by some irrefutable action of miraculous strength, rather similar to the great deliverance in king Hezekiah's day, when the armies of Sennacherib were struck by the breath of the Lord and 185,000 of them destroyed overnight. It was to that sort of dynamic intervention that the Messianic expectations pointed.

The third issue follows on from the teaching Jesus has already given: *How can Christ's disciples be citizens of the king of kings if they are going to be so poor and despised, and are promised so much suffering? Where is the glory of God in that?*

However, throughout all these questions, one factor is becoming increasingly clear, and that is the ever widening divide between those who hear the words of Jesus and prove that by obedience, and those who do not hear because they will not. Chapter 13 explains what is going on as the word of God is being proclaimed in the teaching ministry of Jesus, and also latterly of the disciples. Sowing the seed is defined by Jesus as **'hearing the message about the kingdom'** (verse 19), and the message is about the identity of the king and the rightful claims he makes to rule in the lives of all who hear. This message has a non-negotiable content, which demands a personal response.

Twice in this chapter, Jesus uses Old Testament prophecies to explain his purpose. In verses 14-15 he quotes the narrative of Isaiah's call (Isaiah 6: 9-10) where God explains to the prophet that his ministry will be a declaration of truth that will bring judgment on a people whose ears are heavy and hearts hardened. Indeed, their hearing of God's word will simply confirm them in their rebellion since they will refuse to respond to its demands for repentance. In verse 35, Matthew quotes Psalm 78:2, as a prophecy which Jesus has fulfilled, **'I will open my mouth in parables, I will utter things hidden since the creation of the world.'**

We cannot escape from the fact that there is a deliberate veiling of the secrets of the kingdom by the use of parables, because its arrival is not yet in its fullness. We do not yet see the world-shattering effect that the kingdom will have ultimately. When the king returns in power and glory, that will be the cataclysmic upheaval by which the kingdom will be revealed in all its fullness. But these parables are telling us that at this point the kingdom is secret; it is penetrating like salt and light (in the Sermon on the Mount), or like the yeast here, or growing like the tiny mustard seed. It is therefore appropriate that the teaching method of the kingdom should reflect its growth.

Two things are happening simultaneously. The will of God declared in Old Testament prophecy, as to Isaiah, for example, is being fulfilled and worked out in detail. But on the other hand, the word of the kingdom is confirming the hardened hearts, distracted minds and rebellious wills of those who refuse to believe and receive the message which the king declares. It is therefore highly appropriate that the way in which he teaches should match the response which he knows the teaching will produce. Jesus neither told simple, childish stories for everyone, nor did he deliberately hide the truth from his hearers. If he was doing that, why would he have sent the twelve disciples on mission, in chapter 10?

No, what is happening is that the parables serve to harden the hearts of the hard, but to enlighten those who begin to believe and to follow, those who start to do the will of the Father in heaven. The parables say to us that the kingdom is here in grace, now, and we can enter into it, in a measure, if we hear, understand and do. But if on hearing the word, we harden our hearts and reject the message, each time that happens we are making it harder for ourselves ever to respond positively, in the future. Yet we are to know that this kingdom, which is already here, penetrating the dough, will come in power and judgment one day, and that will be the ultimate judgment (crisis) of every human being.

As with the religious leaders in 8th century Judah, during Isaiah's ministry, so with the Pharisees in the Gospels, there was no real hearing of God's word. Jesus expresses the situation in verse 12: **Whoever has will be given more, and he will have an abundance. Whoever does not have, even what he has will be taken from him.** Because they are resistant and have hardened their hearts, even the privileges which they think they have, as God's covenant people, will be removed from them and given to those who have begun to respond. Indeed, the only way to receive more light is to respond to the light you have already received.

So both groups, those who are hardened and those who are hearing, stand in line of Old Testament fulfilment. Throughout the Old Testament there were those who were wilfully blind, who hardened their hearts, who heard God's voice and rebelled. And there were those like the prophets, who began to see the realities. The disciples stand in that tradition while the Pharisees stand in the tradition of the rejectors. The disciples still have to ask for illumination, **'Explain to us the parable of the weeds in the field'** (verse 36), but they are beginning to see. However, for the crowds, it is Psalm 78:2 all over again.

That Old Testament verse makes the point that the parables of

Jesus are revelatory. They are the means by which things we have already heard and known of are explained to us. In his commentary on the Psalms, Derek Kidner writes, 'It makes the past hold up a mirror to the present and brings its dark sayings to light.' In other words, as the psalm goes on to recount the ways of Israel through the whole of the wilderness period, it is telling us things that we may have heard and known, but it is applying them to us in ways that affect the present. It is penetrating our consciousness. It is not obscure and hidden; they are things we have heard and known.

And the purpose of the parable is not to obscure the truth from this generation. Quite the opposite! 'We will not hide them from our children, we will tell the next generation of the praiseworthy deeds of the LORD' (verse 4). Explaining the meaning of the past for the present is what Psalm 78 is all about, and Jesus in teaching the parables is explaining the meaning of the past for the present too. He is showing these religious, orthodox Jews the line in which they stand, in their rejection of him. He is claiming to be the fulfilment of everything they say they believe in, and he is subversively getting under their skin by these stories, in an attempt to bring them to repent. Presumably there were some who did, but for the most part, their hearts became calloused and the very revelation condemned them because they hardened themselves against it.

We have only to look at the next few verses of the Psalm down to verse 8, to see how remarkably appropriate it is. The message to be declared concerns the statutes God decreed for Jacob and the law he established in Israel (verse 5), 'which he commanded our forefathers to teach their children.' Why is this mirror of the past being held up to the present? Why does Jesus teach in parables? The psalm gives two reasons - so that they will trust God, not forgetting his deeds but keeping his commandments (verse 7), and so that they would not become stubborn and rebellious, disloyal and unfaithful to God (verse 8). But that is exactly where the Pharisees were; testing God, asking for signs, grumbling against Jesus, setting out to kill him - just as their forefathers did to Moses, in the desert. They did not believe what Christ said. They could not accept what he did. They rejected God.

The parables, therefore, are part of the present judgment on this generation, while for those who do respond, they bring light. So, we are not to be surprised if the gospel of the kingdom receives a varied reception. There are plenty of ways in which that seed can perish. There is an enemy who will snatch it away; there are trouble and persecution; there are worries and wealth. What produces the good crop is hearing and understanding, which is exactly what the hardened heart will never do. All the soils were represented in the hearts of the great crowds, who heard Jesus teach that day from the boat, as they are every time the word of God is proclaimed.

The big picture of Matthew 13, then, seems to be as follows. The kingdom of heaven has arrived and it is growing, secretly, but penetratingly. Wherever its message is heard, there is confrontation and division. Those who are deaf and blind confirm it by their stubborn refusal to consider the claims of Jesus, the king, seriously. But while the kingdom is here now, it is also not yet here in its fullness. When that day comes, as it most certainly will, then the seed will be fully grown and there will be no more rejection of the king, simply his rejection of those who have rejected him. That will be the sorting of the fish, good from bad, and the separation of the wheat from the weeds. The sequence of six parables therefore begins and ends with the ultimate reality of the eschatological judgment, the far horizon. That final day is the clear focus of the first parable, of the wheat and weeds, and the last, of the dragnet. The second pair (the mustard seed and the yeast) teach the small beginnings of the kingdom, with its gradual growth and ultimate triumph. They warn the sceptical outsiders not to judge the invisible realities by what is seen. The third pair (the hidden treasure and the pearl) teach the priceless value of membership of the kingdom, far beyond all that one might have in this world. They encourage the sacrificial disciples to know that they have chosen eternal wealth, in following the king.

The delay in the coming of the kingdom

The parable of the Wheat and Weeds (verses 24-30) is a comparatively simple story and we are given our Lord's own interpretation of it in verses 37-43. It is all the more remarkable that the church seems to have consistently misrepresented what Jesus is actually teaching. One of the keys to the parable is his clear statement in verse 38, **The field is the world,** but countless preachers and commentators want to make the field mean the church. We are told that the first century congregations, in which Matthew's Gospel circulated, would be very concerned about false teaching which was beginning to invade them. The parable is then put forward as an example of how we should never aspire to have a pure church, but recognise that there will always be a mixed multitude in the church, and only the Lord can sort that out at the end. He will make the judgments on the last day, and we just have to get on with the job knowing that the wheat and the weeds will grow together. But Jesus said the field is the world, not the church, and the good seed stands for the 'sons of the kingdom'. The kingly reign of Christ is never synonymous with the church, in the synoptic Gospels.

This is a parable which deals with the problem of the delay in the kingdom's full arrival. As Dr. Don Carson puts it, with his customary pithiness, in his commentary on Matthew, 'The parable deals with eschatological expectation, not ecclesiological deterioration.'[3] In other words, it explains how the kingdom can be present now without sweeping everything out of its way, and destroying all its opponents. Do we not need that sort of parable in a generation like ours which is obsessed with power? One of the unrecognised motivations, surely, in the quest for power within the contemporary evangelical church, is that we do not actually believe that a parable like this is true. We want to see the triumph of the kingdom in the here and now. But Jesus denies us that. He says that in the world the sons of the king and the sons of the evil one will exist side by side, until the last day. Far from it being about the church, it is an explanation of why the kingdom is not triumphantly sweeping all before it in the present world order. It will always be that way until the last day when the weeds are pulled up and burned in the fire, and the Son of Man sends out his angels to gather the grain into his barn. That is clearly the focus.

Similarly, the parable of the dragnet, at the end of the sequence, is a parable about that future separation: **'This is how it will be at the end of the age. The angels will come and separate the wicked from the righteous and throw them into the fiery furnace'** (verses 49-50). But only at the end of the age. Because there will be a dividing, therefore you must make your decision now in the light of that, says Jesus. You have chosen the treasure hidden in the field, the pearl of great price, and on that day you will know that it was right. But you may well find in the days in between, that you are tempted, like John the Baptist, to say, 'Is he the one? Have we followed the wrong course?' And you may well find when they persecute you from one city to a next, and when you see apparently very little good soil and a great deal of scorched seed, choked seed and rocky places, you will be tempted to say, 'Was it really worth it?' Disciples will need to be sure not to judge by what they see. They will need to be confident in the eternal values of the king's teaching and aware of the secret penetration of the yeast in the dough.

The growth of the kingdom

That is the nature of the kingdom from which we can take great encouragement in the parable of the mustard seed (verses 31-32). **'Though it is the smallest of all your seeds, yet when it grows, it is the largest of garden plants and becomes a tree, so that the birds of the air come and perch in its branches.'** That's a very vivid picture, isn't it? The mustard seed is, proverbially, the smallest seed. It was cultivated in the rich soil of the Jordan valley and commonly it grew to ten feet or so, into a very substantial bush, or small tree, large enough for birds to come and rest in its branches. Here is the other side of the picture. In spite of all the hindrances and disappointments, in spite of the fact that the work of God seems often to be bedevilled by the enemy's weeds in the world, nevertheless the obscure beginnings are grown by God into a kingdom that expresses his power and glory.

It was true of Jesus himself. Born of a peasant girl in an obscure corner of the Roman empire, cradled in a manger, a refugee in infancy, living insignificantly in Nazareth, nowhere to lay his head, no home to call his own, hounded by those who had influence, murdered on a cross, buried in a borrowed tomb. No one would choose to write a drama or a novel about a great world figure with that kind of background. No, but that is the point about the kingdom of heaven!

The same thing could be said of the disciples. They were ignorant and unlearned men by rabbinic standards, but God used them to turn the world upside down. The same thing could be said of the Reformers, or Whitefield and Wesley - small beginnings. It could be said of any revival, couldn't it? It starts with a number of hearts whom God burdens, with the good news. But there is the life of God in this seed. It is indestructible, so it will grow, as many people in many nations press into it and submit to the authority of Jesus the king.

We may not yet see it growing in our land as we long to see it, but it is growing. Indeed, 'All over the world this gospel is producing fruit and growing, just as it has been doing among you since the day you heard it and understood God's grace in all its truth' (Colossians 1:6). It has to grow; that is the nature of the kingdom. We are not to measure spiritual work by its size, but by its vitality; not by all the trumpet-blowing about how important it is going to be, but by its penetration into the lives of people. Our part is to make sure that we are sowing the good seed of the kingdom. We are looking for real growth, and expecting our God to be at work, even through our lives.

It is that sort of expectation that comes out in the parable of the yeast (verse 33). Here is the method by which God's kingdom grows. Normally, in the Bible, yeast, or leaven, symbolises the penetration of evil, but here the opposite is true. The housewife works the yeast into the dough until the whole batch is affected. That is the kind of change which submitting to the rule of Jesus makes in our lives. It works the authority of Christ into our whole being, not so much in outward form, as in the spirit and character of things.

Because Christ is working like that in individual lives, where you put those individual lives together, they begin to affect the whole community. This is very important with regard to our Christian influence in society. The kingdom of heaven does not come with observation, it is within God's people, like yeast hidden in the dough. It is not an earthly kingdom at all, yet it can penetrate every level and area of society. Although the early church had no great strategy of evangelism, they reached the world because the lives they lived demonstrated a reality of truth and love which was infectious, so that the gospel was caught as well as taught. God's kingly rule is not remote from the world, but hidden in it, to benefit it.

We should be greatly encouraged by that. Perhaps we spend too much time looking at the weeds, though we do need to be realistic about the world in which we live. But there is another side of the coin. God is constantly at work and we never know whose life he may choose to touch through us, if we are prepared to be involved for the kingdom. We cannot compel any human being to accept God's truth, but we can be infectious. That is the means the Holy Spirit often uses, as we mix in the natural units of life. It is a great tragedy when Christians take themselves out of the world into a separatist, little Christian *ghetto*, with no time to meet those who are not yet Christians, so busy doing *church* things that they cannot spread the contagion of the gospel. Is that not why so many people in our society have never actually heard the Christian message?

The value of the kingdom

We can only be content with such a state of affairs if we do not take the last pair of parables equally seriously. In verse 44, Jesus tells us, **'The kingdom of heaven is like treasure hidden in a field. When a man found it, he hid it again, and then in his joy went and sold all he had and bought that field.'** The key note of the story is that the hidden treasure seems to have been found almost by accident. Someone has put it there in the past, presumably for safety, but the sheer joy of the unexpected discovery is the overwhelming impression.

In the second story of the pearl, the merchant discovers the treasure as the result of careful searching. He was looking for fine pearls, perhaps for many years: **'When he found one of great value, he went away and sold everything he had and bought it'** (verse 46). The circumstances were different, but the result was exactly the same. These parables are to assure the disciples of the rightness of their choice, but also to teach them to expect this sort of reaction to the gospel. 'If a man is truly convinced of the importance of the kingdom,' says Bishop Ryle, 'if he is truly convinced of the importance of salvation, he will give up everything to win Christ and eternal life.'

I am not sure we have taken that seriously enough. Do we really value the kingdom that highly? A man becomes a true Christian only because he is thoroughly persuaded that he must. It is not because he says that he can believe that it probably happened, so he supposes he had better trust, but because he knows this is the most important thing he has ever heard. We need that sort of old fashioned Christianity, where the most important thing that we have ever heard is to put the kingly rule of Jesus first, to put off the old life, to leave the world, to count all things as loss for Christ, because we have found the pearl of great price.

Some will find the kingdom almost by chance, as the woman of Samaria did, when she went that day to the well and found Jesus. Some may find him after a long search, as the Ethiopian eunuch did, in the chariot, when he had been trying for so long to find out what the Scriptures meant. Some are like Nathaniel who was waiting so long for the Messiah to come. But whether it is immediately, or after a long search, we have to recognise in Jesus Christ the treasure, the priceless pearl, which is worth absolutely everything. If your heart is that way towards him, you are taking him seriously. But if you are divided in heart, if you say, 'Well, of course, Christianity is interesting, but I want it only in that compartment of my life and I don't want it to affect too much,' then you haven't really yet begun to understand what it is all about.

'**Have you understood all these things?**' Jesus asked his disciples (verse 51). '**Yes**,' they replied. I would love to know what tone of voice they said it in, wouldn't you? He said to them, '**Therefore every teacher of the law who has been instructed about the kingdom of heaven is like the owner of a house who brings out of his storeroom new treasures as well as old**' (verse 52). As the old is fulfilled by the king so the new treasures are revealed by the king, for the members of the kingdom are dependent on their sovereign Lord for every good thing.

8

Live the Truth

The verse with which the parables' discourse ends (13:52) is some-times cited as a summary not only of that chapter, but of the Gospel of Matthew, as a whole. It is certainly a very important bridge in to the second half of the book. However, we are not best served by the NIV translation of this particular text. The teacher of the law instructed in the things of the kingdom, it says, is like a wealthy man, **'who brings out of his storeroom new treasures as well as old'**. But the original literally reads 'new things and old things', which is to say that the new treasures are not tacked on to the old, but take precedence over them. It is not that the old is the major ingredient and the new treasures are added on, but that the two are held together. This is a reading that is very true to the fulfilment theme of Matthew, which we have been tracing all the way from 5:17, **'I have not come to abolish the [law and the prophets] but to fulfil them.'**

We are being taught not so much that there are two testaments which are balanced equally, but that there is one revelation, and its focus now is the new, which has both fulfilled and renewed the old. The Old Testament promises of the prophets and the Old Testament law code running together, both find their fulfilment in Christ the king. Therefore the scribes of the kingdom, that is, those who have been instructed about this truth, will understand that and teach it to others. These are the new and old treasures that are to be passed on from the storeroom of the king.

The growth in the disciples' understanding is one of the themes Matthew is specially wanting to stress at this point of the Gospel. The next few chapters are crucial for that, since it is an essential ingredient for the ordering of the kingdom community which is being formed by this teaching. So clearly the Lord links their new title in verse 52, **'Every teacher of the law who has been instructed about the kingdom of heaven,'** with their new confessed understanding (verse

51). They have the treasure store, the pearl of great price, for which you will sell everything that you possess, but they must always remember that it is the gift of God. In 13:11 Jesus reminded them, **'The knowledge of the secrets of the kingdom of heaven has been given to you, but not to them'** (the crowds). On the basis of that gift, they can come to Jesus and ask him to explain the meaning of the parable (13:36) which he immediately does.

The teaching of Jesus is beginning to gather and to identify a new community. It is a community of those who *understand* and their task will be to teach others the secrets of the kingdom into which they are being initiated. Jesus calls them 'scribes' (literally) as though to emphasise both a fulfilment or continuity with the old Israel, but also a radical discontinuity with its failed religious systems. The new community will require new teachers, just as new wine demands new wine skins. It is not surprising then to find the next major teaching block in chapter 18, towards which we are moving, focusing on the nature of the kingdom community. Nor is it surprising that the intervening chapters, 14-17, highlight the developing division, a division that depends on faith or unbelief, and therefore on understanding or remaining blind.

In 13:53-58, we return to the controversies about the identity of Jesus of Nazareth. Coming to his home town, he began teaching the people in their synagogue, and they were amazed. Yet it is in Nazareth that Jesus finds his own people take offence at him. **'Isn't this the carpenter's son? Isn't his mother's name, Mary, and aren't his brothers James, Joseph, Simon and Judas? Arn't all his sisters with us? Where then did this man get all these things?' And they took offence at him** (verses 54-57). That word *offence* introduces a verb that is going to occur a number of times through these next few chapters; it is the verb, *scandalizo*, which means to cause stumbling, to make someone fall. It links to the stone of stumbling, the rock of offence, as Christ is called later in the New Testament (1 Peter 2:7-8). But the reason for their stumbling is a highly significant one: **And he did not do many miracles there because of their lack of faith** (verse 58). The divisions are beginning to become clearer. This refusal to believe, the lack of faith, is the cause of their stumbling. They stumble over Christ because their eyes are blinded, because **'hearing, they do**

not hear, and seeing, they do not perceive' (13:13). It is a note which will be echoed several times in the next few chapters.

In chapter 14, we have Herod's guilty conscience convincing him that Jesus is John the Baptist, risen from the dead. This presents a view of Jesus so wide of the mark, that it seems at the very opposite end of the belief spectrum. And in contrast to this incredible blindness as to who Jesus is, there follow, in chapter 14, two great signs.

The first, which is the bread from heaven (verses 13ff) or the feeding of the five thousand, may well be taken to indicate a new Moses, sustaining the community of his followers supernaturally, as with the manna in the desert, though that is implicit, I think, rather than emphasised. More likely, the miracle is a partial fulfilment of the promise of the Messianic banquet. In 8:11, Jesus has talked about those from the east and west coming and taking their places at the feast with Abraham, Isaac and Jacob in the kingdom of heaven. Here we have a foretaste of that, and the feeding of the 4,000, later on, augments it. From Isaiah's time onward, there had been a great expectation that one day God would spread the table for his people, when Messiah came to triumph over all his enemies. It is a majestic promise.

> On this mountain the LORD Almighty will prepare a feast of rich food for all peoples, a banquet of aged wine, the best of meats and the finest of wines. On this mountain he will destroy the shroud which enfolds all peoples; the sheet that covers all nations; he will swallow up death for ever. The sovereign LORD will wipe away the tears from all faces; he will remove the disgrace of his people from all the earth. In that day they will say, "Surely this is our God; we trusted in him and he saved us. This is the LORD, we trusted in him; let us rejoice and be glad in his salvation" (Isaiah 25:6-9).

However, one of the most interesting ingredients in the story of the feeding is the comment Jesus makes to the disciples when they present him with the needs of the people and suggest he sends them away to buy food. **"Jesus replied, 'They do not need to go away. You give them something to eat'"** (14:16). In fact, the disciples do give them the food, as they receive the miraculously multiplied loaves and fish from the Lord's hands and pass them on to the people. But they can only give what Christ has first produced and given to them. In this way, the disciples are being trained to be totally dependent on Christ, and the miracle appears to be as much for the disciples to understand and journey further along the road of faith, as it is for the immediate physical needs of the crowd to be satisfied. Although the sign was public, Matthew's focus is on the lesson for the disciples.

The same is certainly true of the second great sign in chapter 14, that of Jesus walking on the water, which is given privately to the disciples expressly to nurture their 'little faith'. After this event they worship him in the boat, ascribing to him for the first time the recognition, **'Truly you are the Son of God'** (14:33). That is what we hear in the voice from heaven when Jesus was baptised at the beginning of the Gospel (3:17). That is how Jesus has described himself in 11:27, when he speaks, as the Son, about his revelation of the Father. And the strand will come to its full development later on, when Peter expresses on behalf of all the disciples the great confession, **'You are the Christ, the Son of the Living God'** (16:16), confirmed by the voice from heaven on the Mount of Transfiguration, **'This is my Son, whom I love; with him I am well pleased. Listen to him!'** (17:5). Ultimately, the confession will even be on the lips of a pagan centurion and his men, at the end of the book, **'Surely he was the Son of God!'** (27:54).

This recognition, which is seen to be the dividing point between the old Israel and the new, is predominantly a matter of faith. And that is also a theme that is well worth tracing through Matthew.

Several times Jesus refers to 'little faith': e.g. **'If that is how God clothes the grass of the field, which is here today and tomorrow is thrown into the fire, will he not much more clothe you, O you of little faith?'** (6:30). He refers to 'great faith' in 8:10 when he heals the centurion's servant: **he was astonished and said to those following him, 'I tell you that I have not found anyone in Israel with such great faith.'** He says to the woman in 9:22, **'Take heart, daughter, your faith has healed you.' And she was healed from that moment;** and to the blind and dumb men in 9:29, **'According to your faith will it be done to you.'** Then, as we come into chapter 15, we find another great faith story, this time with a Canaanite woman (verses 21-28), and Jesus' comment at the end of that story, **'Woman, you have great faith! Your request is granted.' And her daughter was healed from that very hour.** In this case a Gentile woman in Gentile territory is being commended for her faith.

So what is happening? Clearly, the big picture is that the community of faith is being gathered, and that it includes some very unlikely candidates - a Gentile officer, a sick woman, blind men, a Gentile woman living outside Israel. But it also means some even more unlikely exclusions as the unbelievers are also increasingly identifying themselves. The fulfilment of the promise inevitably involves confrontation. Chapter 15:1-20 provides what is perhaps the classic controversy with the Pharisees in the whole of the Gospel, and so for the rest of this chapter, we must focus on what Jesus is teaching through it.

The Pharisees unmasked [1]

One of the staggering conclusions that a dialogue like this forces on us is the realisation that neither the Pharisees nor the people of their day knew how spiritually blind they really were. Worldliness is always very difficult to identify, because it is a hidden root in the heart

---

1. **Then some Pharisees and teachers of the law came to Jesus from Jerusalem and asked, "Why do your disciples break the tradition of the elders? They don't wash their hands before they eat!"**

Jesus replied, "And why do you break the command of God for the sake of your tradition? For God said, 'Honour your father and mother' and, 'Anyone who curses his father or mother must be put to death.' But you say that if a man says to his father or mother, 'Whatever help you might otherwise have received from me is a gift devoted to God,' he is not to 'honour his father' with it. Thus you nullify the word of God for the sake of your tradition. You hypocrites! Isaiah was right when he prophesied about you:

" 'These people honour me with their lips,
> **but their hearts are far from me.**
They worship me in vain;
> **their teachings are but rules taught by man.' "**
Jesus called the crowd to him and said, "Listen and understand. What

long before it expresses itself in outwardly visible behaviour. Moreover, religious behaviour can be just as worldly as the more flagrant hedonistic materialism which we can all readily condemn, because it is centred in self-conceit and the praise of men. No one had a higher doctrine of Scripture, at least in theory, than the Pharisees. Impeccably orthodox in their opinions, remarkably disciplined in their devotion, who would have thought them to be excluded from God's kingdom? Yet, when the Son of God came, he showed them just how far from God they really were. We would be very foolish indeed to write them off and pretend that the same roots of worldliness are not in our own hearts. It is when we see ourselves as the Pharisees, actual and potential, that this dialogue comes alive. We have nothing to boast about. That worldly spirit can still look very sound and very committed, but the wolves that savage God's flock are not usually labelled as such. They always wear sheep's clothing.

Tradition
Firstly, let us look at the charge which the Pharisees lay against Jesus, in verses 1-2. He and his disciples break the tradition of the elders, by not washing their hands before eating. It is instructive to notice how Matthew contrasts that with the end of chapter 14, where Jesus is in the

---

goes into a man's mouth does not make him 'unclean', but what comes out of his mouth, that is what makes him 'unclean'."

Then the disciples came to him and asked, "Do you know that the Pharisees were offended when they heard this?"

He replied, "Every plant that my heavenly Father has not planted will be pulled up by the roots. Leave them; they are blind guides. If a blind man leads a blind man, both will fall into a pit."

Peter said, "Explain the parable to us."

"Are you still so dull?" Jesus asked them. "Don't you see that whatever enters the mouth goes into the stomach and then out of the body? But the things that come out of the mouth come from the heart, and these make a man 'unclean'. For out of the heart come evil thoughts, murder, adultery, sexual immorality, theft, false testimony, slander. These are what make a man 'unclean'; but eating with unwashed hands does not make him 'unclean' " (Matthew 15:1-20 NIV).

very midst of his ministry; people were bringing the sick to him and begging him to let them just touch the edge of his cloak, and all who touched him were healed (verses 35-36). Jesus is being touched by unclean people, and yet from him goes out that healing power, which transforms their lives, physically. Now the Pharisees come with their concern, not about the ministry of Jesus in healing people, but about why his disciples do not ritually wash their hands before meals. It seems as though an official delegation has arrived from the hierarchy in Jerusalem. The top men are working on their report and they have a key question to ask, or rather a basic charge to bring: 'You, Jesus of Nazareth, break the tradition of the elders.'

Of course, this has nothing to do with hygiene and everything to do with ceremonial, ritual purification. The tradition of the elders was that your hands had to be plunged into water, up to the wrist, and vessels had to be thoroughly washed before you could eat anything. To neglect this was to be guilty, the elders said, of gross defilement. So, one of the rabbis said that bread eaten with unwashed hands is as if it is filth. Clearly, Jesus knew that, but he also knew that his disciples were under the most careful scrutiny. So, as their teacher, he must have instructed them to act in this way. He must have deliberately precipitated this controversy because he wanted to move beyond the surface criticisms that the Pharisees were constantly lobbing at him, to the underlying problems, which he exposes in this dialogue.

For the Pharisees it is a clear case of their oral traditions being infringed. Those traditions were passed on and elaborated over the centuries before Christ. They were not written in the Scriptures, but the Pharisees taught that they had been given to Moses by God on Mount Sinai, in addition to the law. Jesus uses this whole controversy to expose, and to teach to the disciples the deeper issue, which is not one of ceremonial ritual at all, but one of Biblical authority. Are the traditions of the elders to be obeyed, as the written Scriptures are to be obeyed? Do they have the imprimatur of divine authority? What is really at stake here, you could say, in contemporary terms, is the sufficiency of God's self-revelation in Scripture, the sufficiency of the Bible.

Most evangelicals are generally quite good at finding heresy that cuts things out of the Bible; indeed many of us have been trained in that way. We know how to spot when critics come to Scripture and cut out things that are clearly an integral part of the divine revelation. So when we have the Bible minus the incarnation, or minus the bodily resurrection, or minus the supernatural, we spot it instantly and we rightly label it as heresy.

But there is an equally great danger in the *Bible-plus*, which we do not spot so readily. This is because its exponents assert that they really do accept and believe the whole Bible. That is what every Pharisee would have asserted about the Old Testament law. Every word was inspired, but they added to it the words of men, and by doing that they effectively destroyed its authority.

As a twentieth century parallel take the following pronouncement of the Roman Catholic Church following the second Vatican Council: 'Sacred tradition and sacred scripture form one sacred deposit of the word of God which is committed to the church.' It is an exact replica of Matthew 15. Here are two different authorities, sacred scripture (the divine authority) and sacred tradition (the human authority), which is actually put first in the statement, merged into one, in order to prepare the way for totally unbiblical doctrines to be accepted and promulgated on the basis that this is the sacred deposit of the truth committed to the church. The *Bible-plus* ultimately destroys the Bible.

There are some circles today where prophecies and 'words of wisdom' and 'knowledge' are given publicly in terms of 'Thus says the Lord...' or 'I say to you, my people...'. The question with any such pronouncement, whether by an elder, or apostle (as such people sometimes call themselves), or even by the whole leadership of a church or fellowship, is what authority it is to have. If this really is a word from God, ought it not to be on a par with the authority of the written word in Scripture? But as soon as you accept that, you immediately have the *Bible-plus*, and the word of the contemporary prophet will eventually always seem to be more urgent, or powerful, or relevant than the written word. So, again, Scripture is down-graded for the new authority of 'the Bible plus the prophet' as though 'God's word in Scripture' was insufficient in itself. Sadly, we all know how this can lead to a sectarian, cultic extremism, which in the end even denies the gospel. To their credit, many wise leaders in such fellowships today are concerned not to claim too much authority for these extra-biblical utterances. It would be helpful if this logic was followed through and such 'words' were clearly distinguished from the authoritative word of God.

Or, there are Biblical, evangelical churches which are practically ruled by all sorts of traditions, mainly unwritten, and all the more strongly cherished for that reason. They are the ones that the outsider stumbles over first of all so that he very quickly realises that he is an outsider. 'We don't do it that way here; we don't think in those terms.' It is not a matter of Biblical truth, it is a matter of tradition. When these traditions actually govern the practice of the church, they ensure that we get stuck in the concrete of outdated cultural norms, so that in the world's eyes the church becomes more and more a fossil of a bygone age.

We elevate our traditions above the word of God. We would claim to be Bible-believing Christians, but in such situations, we are *Bible-plus* Christians, when it comes to authority. We have added our traditions as an extra level of control, and the greatest casualty is the gospel. Keeping the rules becomes more important than rescuing the lost. And, of course, as we turn in more and more on ourselves and our systems, we become increasingly disappointed, fractious and fragmented. As someone remarked to me recently about church life, 'If we are not fishing, we shall be fighting.' Church history is full of examples of that principle being worked out.

Adding to the Word

In verses 3-6, we come to Jesus' reply, which is the form of a counter-charge. He exposes the *Bible-plus* attitude as the very heart of Pharisaism and his concern is especially directed at the two totally destructive effects that it has. To break the command of God for the sake of your tradition is actually to elevate yourself above God (verse 3) and this means, secondly, that you **'nullify the Word of God'** (verse 6). If the Bible is not the chief authority in your life, you have robbed it of its power and nullified its effect. The particular one that Jesus underlines in verses 4-6 helps us to grasp the general principle.

There is no doubt in Jesus' mind that what the Bible says, God says. "For God said, 'Honour thy father and thy mother'" (verse

4). He is quoting, of course, from the ten commandments. And, **"Anyone who curses his father or mother must be put to death,"** again quoting from the book of Leviticus. Jesus says that is the word of God. What Scripture says, God says. The whole of Scripture is God revealing his mind and will to his people.

You find this emphasis throughout Christ's ministry, and it is one of the major reasons why we accept the Old Testament as the inspired word of God. It is a logical conclusion of our submission as disciples of Jesus Christ to him as Lord, that what our Lord believed about the Old Testament, we believe about the Old Testament. So, the teaching of the Old Testament law was quite specific. It is not Moses making it up; it is from God. Here, then, is what God says about family life and about family responsibilities, and in this specific context, especially about respect and care for parents.

But the Pharisees had added specific regulations to this. For example, you could put your money into a special temple fund, which was devoted to God for religious purposes and if you vowed your money in that way, it was, as Mark tells us in his Gospel, using a technical term, *corban* - set apart for God. Because that was a vow, there was no going back on it, according to the Pharisees, and not one penny of the money could be used for any other purpose. If you had elderly parents who were in need, in a situation where there was no welfare state to assist in old age or sickness, that was just too bad! It was *corban*. And, of course, if you just wanted to designate that money as being *corban* but kept it in your account, it gave you an excellent excuse for not using any of it on your parents.

This provides Jesus with a crystal clear example of how they domesticated the thrust of God's word, by adding to it a tradition, which relied entirely on men for its authority. It kept them comfortable. They were able to keep that law, because they hedged it around with so many qualifications, and man-made additions. Instead of the law of God penetrating their hearts, convicting them of their sinful nature, and then driving them to Christ for his mercy and his grace, they became proud of what they thought they were able to do, thinking that they accepted the divine revelation, but actually domesticating it by their traditions. So, when the Lord of glory offered his grace, they turned their backs on him; they didn't need it.

Hypocrisy

At verse 7, Jesus deepens and broadens his analysis of the Pharisees' plight. Using a quotation from Isaiah 29:13 he exposes the hypocrisy of their attitude. In his context, Isaiah is denouncing the false prophets and the clueless teachers of his day, who cannot understand the clear word of God. This state of ignorance exists because they have refused to respond to the light they had. They honoured God with their lips, but their hearts were not where their lips were. Their worship was in vain, because instead of following the word of God they were following the rules of men. It was man-made religion which thrives whenever we elevate human rules above God's word, or put external conformity above heart-religion. The issue Jesus addresses is firstly one of heart integrity before God.

It is still possible for us as Christian believers to be saying all the right things, singing God's praises, expressing worship and honour to him in prayer; and yet for our hearts all the time to be hardening, to be cold, because they are turning away from the living God. We can be caught up in worship; we can formulate correct doctrine; we can discuss all the latest Christian ideas; and yet the whole ethos can be empty and bogus, merely human, if we do not have a heart that is on fire with love for God. The heart of the human problem is always the problem of the human heart. The real issue is always the inner life rather than mere outward conformity. But there is only one power that can change the heart, as we are taught by implication in the quotation from Isaiah. That happens when the word of God is being received and obeyed, rather than the teaching and traditions of men, which is why the Pharisees were in such problems. Their adherence to their own rules, to the club system, was thoroughly worldly, and Jesus challenges them to the depth of their beings as he calls the crowd to him to make the issue one hundred per cent clear. **"But the things that come out of the mouth come from the heart, and these make a man 'unclean' "** (verse 18).

That is why I said they were 'worldly' because this world is only interested in the outward appearance, the image rather than the substance. This world's concern lies in what other people think, how envious or critical they are, not in what God sees or how God judges. And whenever we elevate our human rules to a position of authority, we become worldly and start to nullify the word of God. To live by the traditions of men is powerless and destructive, because it eventually leads to a hardened heart.

Sadly, I have met Christians who seem to have learned hardly anything, who have not grown or changed, in thirty or forty years. They still take you back to what they learned in the Youth Fellowship when they were eighteen, and they have never moved further than that. Their heart seems to have hardened out completely. How does that happen? By doing nothing. All I have to do to make my heart hard is to do nothing at all. If I just allow the natural process of my sinful human nature to drift me away from the word of God, my heart will become hardened, as will yours.

We have to do something about it, because unless we are actively seeking to grow in godliness, to become more like Jesus, to be obedient to God's word, day by day, we shall just stay still. Our Christian lives will begin to seize up. But what the world needs to see is a people whose heart and lips are at one, in a genuine devotion to God, a consistent honouring of the king. That is to be the calling of the new covenant community.

In recent years, the ministry of Willow Creek Community Church in a residential area of greater Chicago has become very widely known. One of the largest and fastest growing churches in the USA, its philosophy is summed up by the senior pastor, Bill Hybels, as providing 'a church for the unchurched'. I remember an older Christian saying to me, 'But that's impossible. The church is for God, not for the unconverted.' Theologically it is true that the glory of God and the riches of his mercy are nowhere more clearly displayed in this world than in the church he died to redeem. But why does he keep his people in this world? What is the church to be doing? Is it not to be the world's salt and light, a city set on a hill that cannot be hidden? And if that is so, then to have a heart after God's heart must be to have a heart for lost people, because 'they matter to God'. If I have no concern for those outside of Christ, particularly the thousands of young people who are totally without any Christian friends or influences, can I really say that my heart is beating in time with God's heart? All too often I've been content with my membership of the Pharisees' club and all too unaware of how quickly my heart becomes hardened.

All this happened in the Pharisees' experience, because instead of sitting under the authority of Scripture day by day, and letting the word of God judge and divide the heart, bringing a conviction that leads to repentance, they elevated their own traditions and blunted the sword of the Spirit, so that its point never reached their hearts. But Jesus says this will not go on for ever: **'Every plant that my heavenly Father has not planted will be pulled up by the roots. Leave them; they are blind guides'** (verses 13-14). We need to set the word of God loose, to do its real and lasting work in our lives. It is not always a pleasant experience, but it is essential. When we hold the mirror of God's word up to our lives, we can instantly recognise the things that make us unclean. Verse 19 is not just about the Pharisees, it is about us: **'For out of the heart come evil thoughts, murder, adultery, sexual immorality, theft, false testimony, slander. These are what makes a man "unclean".'**

When we see ourselves in the light of that, then we realise what sinners we are, and why we constantly need to submit ourselves to the word of God, to run to the Christ of God for his cleansing so that by the power of his Holy Spirit we might live lives that are different. Not lives that are keeping another set of rules, but lives that are opened up to the revolutionising power of the Holy Spirit, who changes us from the inside out. It will mean that we have a resolute commitment to God's revealed word in every aspect and area of our lives. We are not at liberty to pick and choose. We shall want to sit under its authority and seek to be obedient in every part of our being and in all our relationships. It may mean a radical restructuring of much of our time and priorities, so that we become more orientated to those who do not yet know the good news of the kingdom. When the holiness that God is working in us gets lived out in the world, then the world sees spiritual reality and begins to get hungry.

It will mean that we break out of our comfort zones where we go 'low profile' so that nobody knows that we are Christians, and we start to stand up for Jesus, and not be ashamed of him. We take him seriously. It means that in our church life we ask one another, 'What are we doing to reach the thousands of people all around us?' We believe that the preaching of the word is the divine means by which God convicts of sin and brings men and women to salvation, but what are we doing to bring them to hear the word preached? And if they are the sort of people for whom the transition to church is too demanding as a first step, what are we doing to help them along that road? Are we prepared to open our homes? Are we prepared to spend time with individuals? Are we prepared to set up little basic Christianity discovery groups, evangelistic Bible Studies, or whatever is appropriate to the people? We have to think in those terms when once we start to take Jesus seriously.

It will mean a personal availability to God, to live authentic lives of trust and obedience. 'Here I am, wholly available. As for me, I will serve the Lord.' If we sit under his word, allowing him to show us what is unclean, then repenting of our sin and finding his fresh cleansing, we can ask him every day to use us for his greater purposes.

In October 1989 a church census was taken of as many congregations as would respond throughout England, and tens of thousands did. As a result of that inquiry it became clear that over the decade 1979-89, church attendance decreased at a weekly average of 1,000 people. Some of them went to heaven, for which we can only rejoice, but the staggering fact is that 600 out of the 1,000 were teenagers. 600 young people were leaving our churches every week for a decade. Could it be that they discovered that few of those who remained were really taking Jesus seriously?

9

Practise the Principles

'Do you know that the Pharisees were offended when they heard this?' This question to Jesus by the disciples in 15:12 may strike us as a little naive. It certainly shows something of the respect, and even fear, in which the religious leaders were held by ordinary people like the Twelve. It is also a warning of what is to come. No-one offended a Pharisaical delegation from Jerusalem with impunity. But Jesus knew precisely what he was doing.

Now, in the privacy of his conversation with his followers (the new Israel) he takes up two of the metaphors which the Pharisees habitually used to describe themselves - 'the Lord's planting' and 'the guides of the blind' (15:13-14). Because the nation was described as the Lord's vine, the work of his hands and the product of his care, they thought of themselves as the flower of that plant, the guardians of all that was distinctive in covenant life. But for Jesus, they are like the weeds of chapter 13, which will eventually have to be pulled up. By their fruits of pride and unbelief, they demonstrate that the heavenly Father has not planted them. Because of their custodianship of the Torah (the law) they called themselves the guides of the blind, but in failing to see Christ as its fulfilment, they reveal themselves to be blind. All they can do is lead the people into a pit. The division is becoming increasingly clear, which is why the story of a Gentile woman who does believe follows on immediately and is so poignant (15:21-28).

To the Pharisee, she was doubly insignificant. They would not teach the law to a woman, or even allow her to sit at a rabbi's feet. She was also a Gentile, far from the covenant provision, and beyond the sphere of God's interest. But she is a Gentile woman who recognises Jesus as the Lord, the Son of David (verse 22). So, although Christ's first priority is to provide the children (the lost sheep of Israel) with bread, even the dogs (a common Jewish description of the Gentiles) eat the crumbs that fall from the master's table (verse 27). **'Woman, you have great faith!'** is Jesus' response and her daughter is healed (verse 28). Grace is reaching out to bring the outsiders, from all the points of the compass, to the heavenly banquet.

And not just in terms of a few crumbs! 15:29-39 records the second great feeding miracle, when 4,000 men, besides women and children, are miraculously fed from the disciples' food. The significant factor here is that these are Gentile people. For although Matthew refers simply to the Sea of Galilee, in Mark 7:31 we are told that it was the eastern shore to which Jesus came, to the ten cities (the Decapolis) which marked the start of the Gentile world. This is further reinforced by the people's reference to **the God of Israel** (verse 31). Here, then, we have a record of a fairly extensive Gentile ministry. The old order is passing and Israel's time of priority is almost over. The first fruits of the Gentiles are beginning to be gathered.

Chapter 16 shows us why this is so. **'The Pharisees and Sadducees came to Jesus and tested him by asking him to show them a sign from heaven'** (verse 1). As the passage develops, Jesus warns his disciples against **'the yeast of the Pharisees'** (verse 6) which Matthew explains means their teaching (verse 12). The only sign these blind guides will receive is the sign of Jonah (verse 4). This seems to have a double significance. Firstly, Jonah was a prophet specifically sent to the Gentiles, which is clearly a dominant theme in this part of the Gospel. Secondly, it is a sign of resurrection, and Jesus is teaching that faith ultimately rests not on his miracles but on his dying and rising again. It is the mark of that generation, always refusing to believe and demanding more evidence, that it is **wicked and adulterous**. In 17:17, Jesus describes it further as **unbelieving and perverse**, and in that context, following his self-revelation on the Mount of Transfiguration, he even includes the disciples, because they have **so little faith** (17:20).

In between, we have Peter's confession, the first Passion prediction and the Transfiguration itself. Here is the confession of the disciples' faith, followed by the clarification of their faith as Jesus tells them he is going to be a Messiah who will die and be raised on the third day, and the confirmation of their faith in the revelation on the mountain. And yet, it is an understanding that is far from complete or perfect. So, as the two communities are being defined, they are not static; there are people moving between them. And at the end of chapter 17, they confront one another as the prelude to the fourth teaching passage, which is chapter 18.

Arriving in Capernaum, Jesus and the disciples are questioned as to whether he pays the temple tax. There is a very interesting exchange between Jesus and Peter in 17:25-27. Jesus asks him:

> **'From whom do the kings of the earth collect duty and taxes - from their own sons, or from others?'**
>
> **'From others,' Peter answered.**
>
> **'Then the sons are exempt,' Jesus said to him. 'But so that we may not offend them, go to the lake and throw out your line. Take the first fish you catch, open its mouth and you will find a four-drachma coin. Take it and give it to them for my tax and yours.'**

This little incident provides an important bridge into chapter 18

The two drachma tax was levied on every male Jew for the support of the temple and its ministry. Of course, you would expect Peter to be in favour of that. He was the closest follower of the most popular, young rabbi Israel had seen in years. But, not for the last time, Peter gets it wrong. Jesus corrects his understanding, by pointing out that if the kings of the earth do not tax their own sons, then he must be exempt from the temple tax, because he is the unique Son of the heavenly Father. This is what Peter has just confessed him to be: **'You are the Christ, the Son of the Living God'** (16:16). If that is so, then he had better work out its implications for the new kingdom community more carefully. He is a member of the king's household, which makes him exempt too. But because the old is co-existing with the new at this point in time, Jesus tells Peter to go and pay the tax with a coin which will be miraculously provided.

All this has been leading us to the fourth teaching block (chapter 18) which expounds and develops the question of relationships within the new community of the kingdom. It is introduced, in verse 1, by a question which follows on directly from the incident we have just considered: **'Who then** (the *then* is important in the original) **is the**

greatest in the kingdom of heaven?' We know from elsewhere in
the Gospels that this was a subject of some concern to the disciples.
Mrs Zebedee is going to come with her request in 20:20-21, for her
two boys to sit on either side of the Lord in the kingdom. Peter has
been congratulated on his confession of Jesus in 16:17, and then
rebuked six verses later. Three have been selected to see Christ's
glory on the Mount of Transfiguration, but they had all been rebuked
for their lack of faith later on. If Jesus is the Son who does not need
to pay the temple tax, because he is the Lord, what is the disciples'
position? How do they relate to the kingdom? Does their relationship
with the king guarantee them special privileges? Will they be the
'cabinet' when the kingdom comes? How will the new community of
faith be regulated? Who then is the greatest in the kingdom of heaven?

The church
Before we look at the answer Jesus gives, we need to establish this
central idea, that there is to be a continuing community of Christ's
followers. He actually calls it 'the church', the *ecclesia*, in 18:17. This
verse and 16:18 are the only two usages of that word in the Gospels.

It is common, of course, to suggest that its use was an invention
of the Matthean community later on in the first century. Contemporary critics are not slow to make their case that the charismatic,
Galilean, holy man would have been horrified to see the church of the
last twenty centuries, being built on his sayings. That is all blamed on
the apostle Paul. They hold that Jesus' belief in the imminent end of
all things meant that there was neither time nor room in his thinking
for any concept of an organised community of followers, after his life-
time. Whereas Jesus had foretold the kingdom what happened was the
church.

The one positive value in thinking like that is that it separates the
kingdom from the visible church, which must be right. We cannot
equate the rule of God with the authority of the church and its leaders.
But we must not allow that to blind us to the fact that Jesus did foresee
and plan for a continuing community of people who owned him as
Christ, the king. It is happening throughout this Gospel. As we trace
those themes through we can see that the community is inevitably
beginning to be formed.

Howard Marshall puts it with his characteristic good Biblical sense:

> 'The concept of the kingdom of God implies a community. While it has been emphasised almost ad nauseam that the primary concept is that of sovereignty, or kingship, or actual rule of God, and not of a territory ruled by a king, it must also be emphasised that kingship cannot be exercised in the abstract, but only over a people. The concept of the kingship of God implies both the existence of a group of people who own him as king, and the establishment of a realm of people within which his gracious power is manifested.'[4]

The fulfilment theme helps us to understand this. In the first instance, the message of the kingdom is primarily directed to Israel. The opportunity exists to become a member of the renewed community, through the repentance of individuals under John's ministry and through the acceptance of Christ, as he declares the inbreaking of the kingdom. That opportunity is always there, in the Gospel pages. But as Matthew's Gospel unfolds, and we see the Israel of his day increasingly rejecting the Christ, then the theme of judgment predominates. The warnings are there from the beginning but they come to a clearer focus as the Gospel proceeds.

In 19:28 Jesus says to his disciples, '**I tell you the truth, at the renewal of all things, when the Son of Man sits on his glorious throne, you who have followed me will also sit on twelve thrones, judging the twelve tribes of Israel**.' The old Israel will be judged by the new. Indeed, their faith is already a judgment on Israel's unbelief which will be solemnly pronounced at the renewal of all things, when the old Israel is judged by the Son through his disciples.

It is not surprising that Jesus spoke of his disciples as constituting an *ecclesia*, a community of called out people. Nor is it surprising that he uses the term first immediately following Peter's confession of him, '**You are the Christ, the Son of the living God**' (16:16). '**I tell you that you are Peter, and on this rock I will build my** *ecclesia*, **and the gates of Hades will not overcome it. I will give you the keys of the kingdom of heaven; whatever you bind on earth will be**

**bound in heaven, and whatever you loose on earth will be loosed
in heaven.**' And this is paralleled in 18:18, '**I tell you the truth,
whatever you bind on earth will be bound in heaven, and whatever you loose on earth will be loosed in heaven.**' Both times Jesus
refers to the community, he gives that particular promise.

We also need to remember that the term *ecclesia* already had a
well attested history. It is used in the Septuagint, the Greek version of
the Old Testament, of the whole assembly of Yahweh, the people of
God who are his *ecclesia*. The root verb means 'to call out from'. This
has obvious Exodus inferences, which run all through Old Testament
thinking. In the inter-testamental period, it came to be used of a local
congregation, a synagogue where the law was listened to and held in
reverence. It could be used of a crowd of people gathered for a specific
purpose. It is therefore used of the whole nation, what we would
describe as the old Israel. Indeed, it is used that way in the New
Testament itself. In Stephen's great speech in Acts 7, he talks about
the *ecclesia* in the desert, the church in the desert, referring to the
Exodus community.

So when Jesus talks about *my ecclesia*, he is stressing both
fulfilment and discontinuity. The faithful remnant who believe the
new revelation are the fulfilment of all that the old Israel foreshadowed and might have been. But they are distinct, because the old
Israel has become a faithless, unbelieving, increasingly hostile people. So, says Jesus, 'I will build my Israel, my church, my new people,
my kingdom community, and even the powers of death, will not prove
stronger than that building. This will be an everlasting community
that cannot be destroyed.'

Statements like that put Jesus unequivocally in the place of God.
He is claiming in this pronouncement to be the Christ, the Son of God,
the Messiah. The new community is his community. As God is the
king of Israel, so Jesus is the king of the new Israel, and membership
is secured only by relationship to him, by those who declare, 'You are
the Christ, the Son of the living God.' This also helps to explain the
meaning of the difficult references to the keys of the kingdom, and to
binding and loosing. It has been well established that the rabbis used
the metaphors of binding and loosing to mean declaring forbidden
and permitted. Because of its association with the keys, it has been

suggested that Jesus sees it as excluding from or giving entrance to his new *ecclesia*. Both together seem to make the best sense.

Because Christ's emphasis is on the radical newness of the church, Peter and the disciples would never think of themselves as just an alternative sect within Judaism, though, interestingly, that is how the Roman Imperial authorities first regarded the infant church. The disciples knew that they were distinctively different, the new Israel. Yet, they retained the Old Testament Scriptures and lived in the social context of first century Judaism. There would therefore be a continuing need for guidance in the ordering of the practical affairs of the new community, which the disciples are to accept as their responsibility, under the authority of the king. Their ministry of the gospel will make clear the terms of entrance to the kingdom of heaven and their regulation of the church will equally be guided by God. The tenses of the verbs are future perfect, 'shall have been bound' or 'shall have been loosed', indicating that 'as the church is responsive to the guidance of God it will come to the decisions that have already been made in heaven. In John 20:22-23 it is made clear that this is because of the gift of the Holy Spirit' (Leon Morris).

Valuing each other

With this necessary background understanding, we can now appreciate how totally wrong-footed the disciples' question, in 18:1, really was. The values of God's kingdom are in fact diametrically opposed, both to the Gentile kingdoms of this world and to the perversion of Old Testament theology, which the religious leaders of Jesus' day were teaching. The disciples' thinking has every reason to be confused. Jesus has told them that '**there has not risen anyone greater than John the Baptist**' but added '**yet he who is least in the kingdom of heaven is greater than he**' (11:11). If John the Baptist was the 'Elijah' who was promised before the Messiah (Malachi 4:5) as 17:11-13 makes clear he was, then the Old Testament prophetic ministry has come to its fruition, it has been completed. If the disciples are greater than John, who will be the greatest among the great when the kingdom comes in its fullness?

Jesus' answer is to have a little child stand among them as an object lesson and to say, '**I tell you the truth, unless you change and** become like little children, you will never enter the kingdom of heaven' (verse 3). God's system of evaluation is radically different from ours. Commentating on this verse, Dick France says, 'A child was a person of no importance in Jewish society; subject to the authority of his elders; not taken seriously except as a responsibility; one to be looked after, not to be looked up to.' If we take each of those qualifications and think about them, it is pretty devastating, isn't it? But Jesus says that unless we become like that, we cannot even enter the kingdom. Christ's answer is not so much in terms of innocence or humility, though he does speak of humbling oneself, in the next verse. They have asked him a question about status and he confers on them the status of a child, which in Jewish terms meant no status at all. That is the way into the kingdom; it is for the spiritually bankrupt (5:3).

Then, with the little child still standing in the midst, as an inescapable example, Jesus continues in verse 5, '**And whoever welcomes a little child like this in my name welcomes me.**' This begins a new unit of thought, moving away from self-examination to our attitude to one another. I think it would help us to understand it if we were to hyphenate together 'a-little-child-like-this', as one title. It is a description of what it means to be a little one in the kingdom; a humble believer, a true disciple. Jesus is not talking about little children in the physical sense, but about a-little-child-like-this, a humbled Christian who takes no status. That is what it means to be in the kingdom, and so that is the basis of fellowship in the new community. In welcoming one another like that, in the fellowship of his church, we welcome Christ.

'In his name' means that for his sake and submitting to his lordship, we have accepted our own lack of status before God and recognised that we are entirely dependent on his grace. That in turn sets us free to accept one another, as we stand equal before God, recipients of his undeserved mercy. But if we do not, if we entertain ideas about our own importance or status we shall cause other Christians to 'sin' (verse 6) or a better translation is to 'stumble' (the verb is *scandalizo* again) which is such a heinous fault that death by drowning would be preferable. They are strong words, but they illustrate how strongly Jesus felt about the priorities of his new covenant community.

How often we are caught out by Christ's teaching! Christian leaders are often talking about 'ordinary' Christians, in a detached, even slightly superior way, or about the 'average church member'. But each 'little one' is infinitely precious to God. What about the young and immature within our church communities? Are they really welcome and cared for by those who exercise leadership? People come to a new church, 'bright-eyed and bushy-tailed'; perhaps they are newly converted people, and what do they find? So often they discover ladders they have to climb before they are accepted. But Jesus is saying that really denies the very heart of his gospel. It is back to Pharisaism, isn't it? I was talking to a teenager recently who was sharing with me something of her disappointment. She had been to camp in the summer and was thrilled to bits when into her church, one Sunday, came a couple of her camp leaders. She went bounding up to them to say 'Hello' but they looked past her and went straight over to their friends, whom they had really come to see. And she said, 'Well, it shows I am not important. I don't really matter. They said I did at camp, but they didn't mean it.' **If anyone causes one of these little ones to** *stumble.* It is very penetrating, and really is that serious, to Jesus.

Stumbling is all too easy in this world, but when it is caused by the self-centredness of other Christians, it is nothing short of tragic. There will be plenty of things in the world that cause people to sin (stumble) verse 7 says, but we cannot allow the Christian community to have that effect as well. Indeed, we must be merciless with everything within ourselves that might cause us to stumble, and fall away from Christ (verses 8-9). For members of the kingdom, a thorough-going repudiation of all that is offensive to God is a mark of real discipleship. The eternal perspective must govern all of our earthly actions, since the whole of life is lived before the all-seeing eye of God, and these destinies of heaven or hell are both real and both dependent on this life.

Verses 10-14 underline that theme.

See that you do not look down on one of these little ones. For I tell you that their angels in heaven always see the face of my Father in heaven.

> **What do you think? If a man owns a hundred sheep, and one of them wanders away, will he not leave the ninety-nine on the hills and go to look for the one that wandered off? And if he finds it, I tell you the truth, he is happier about that one sheep than about the ninety-nine that did not wander off. In the same way your Father in heaven is not willing that any of these little ones should be lost.**

Jesus' great emphasis, here, is on the preciousness of the individual 'little one', who has no status, but is greatly loved by God. Does verse 10 mean that we each have a guardian angel? The Jerusalem church, praying for the release of Peter, certainly thought that Rhoda had answered the door to his angel (Acts 12:15). But this is not perhaps exactly what Jesus meant. Another interpretation suggests that the angels are the spirits of believers after death, in, heaven, always seeing the Father's face. The comparison is made by Jesus himself in 22:30. In assessing this view, D. A. Carson concludes that 'the evidence, though not overwhelming, is substantial enough to suppose that "their angels" simply refers to their continued existence in the heavenly Father's presence'.[5] Certainly, Jesus is making the point that each individual believer is of infinite value to God and that is the focus of the parable of the lost sheep which follows (verses 12-14).

Here is a 'little one' who is being stumbled, is wandering off, and in danger of being lost. Because each one is of infinite value to the Father, so our role in the new community is to go to the rescue, to protect the little one, to search for the lost, just as the shepherds in Ezekiel 34 should have done, in the old Israel.

That is the way we are to relate to one another in Christ's kingdom. The disciples' question is utterly wrong. It is asking about all the wrong issues. Ours is a ministry of care, because we have no status. It is a ministry of welcome of all on the same ground, because we are all equal before God. It is a ministry of being concerned that we do not cause others, or ourselves, to stumble and fall.

Dealing with problems
But what about when the offence is reversed, when you are the one sinned against?

If your brother sins against you, go and show him his fault, just between the two of you. If he listens to you, you have won your brother over. But if he will not listen, take one or two others along, so that 'every matter may be established by the testimony of two or three witnesses'. If he refuses to listen to them, tell it to the church; and if he refuses to listen even to the church, treat him as you would a pagan or a tax collector (18:15-17).

Here is an all too familiar situation where there is a breakdown of loving relationships between Christian brothers and sisters in God's family, within the kingdom community. Such a set of circumstances is fraught with danger and can lead to all sorts of fragmentation and bitter disputing, if it is not dealt with carefully and Biblically. In breaking a log-jam like this, the important thing is to have one's overall aim clearly defined. Jesus does that for us in verse 15; it is to win your brother over to your way of thinking.

It is important to remember that the stages passed through in these verses all have that end in view, just as the purpose and goal of all disciplinary action within the church is restoration and renewal. It is our responsibility before God to practise these principles, yet in so many church fellowships they seem to be studiously ignored.

The first step, Jesus says, when I have been sinned against by a fellow-Christian is to take the initiative, go to my brother and point out the issue to him, so that things can be rectified; not to go first to someone else and spill it all out to them! What a difference it would make in church life if we agreed to work at this together. It will mean that when someone comes to me to complain about the misdeeds of a fellow Christian, I shall have to stop them, and ask them if they have talked to him face to face about the matter, and refuse to discuss it until that is done, and then only if he is present. Gossip is stopped, at a stroke. Can you imagine the confidence and relaxation that would prevail in a fellowship, if we all knew that talking about others behind their backs was 'out', because none of us would allow one another to do it? Not even complaining obliquely about others 'just for your prayers' would be tolerated.

If this fails, then Jesus follows the Old Testament pattern of sanctioning two or three witnesses; and if this semi-private approach also fails to solve the problems, then the matter is to be brought out into the open and told to the church. They are not easy principles to adopt because they cut across both human pride and fear, but they are to be taken seriously because loving, forgiving relationships among his people are of paramount importance to the king. They are to reflect his relationship with us, which is the only ground for our membership in the kingdom. They are very practical too.

The unwillingness to forgive is a major cause of psychological breakdown, and there is little doubt that a bitter spirit is a killer. It kills the spiritual life of those who cherish it; it kills their emotional, mental and even sometimes their physical health; and it kills the fellowship where it is not dealt with. That is why the plurals of verse 18, which we noted in the passage following Peter's confession in chapter 16, are now seen to indicate action by the church as a whole: '**I tell you the truth, whatever you** (plural) **bind on earth**', said in the singular to Peter in 16:19, is here spoken in the plural to the disciples, as representative of the whole *ecclesia*: '**and whatever you** (plural) **loose on earth will be loosed in heaven.**' The church is able to be authoritative in declaring what is accepted and what is not as the basis of Christ's teaching because heaven has acted first in revealing the gospel, through Christ the Lord. That gospel of God's grace, on which the church is built, is an outcrop of the everlasting kingdom which will one day be revealed in all its glory and completion.

That is the context of verses 19-20:

> **Again, I tell you that if two of you on earth agree about anything you ask for, it will be done for you by my Father in heaven. For where two or three come together in my name, there am I with them.**

These verses are often divorced from their context to make them promises for times of corporate prayer. But the prayer-meeting is not their primary focus, is it? **Anything you ask for** is actually a translation of a phrase that can mean 'any judicial matter', any matter that is currently under dispute, which seems to refer it back very clearly to the preceding verses and their context of resolving controversies and reconciling differences. That interpretation removes it from the prayer-meeting setting altogether, although its truth obviously applies to our praying together. The **two of you** then, in verse 19, are the offender and the offended. If they agree on the matter they are pursuing, it will literally 'succeed', in heaven. It will be ratified by the Father in heaven, who has revealed his kingdom rules for the kingdom community. What Jesus seems to be saying is that this confirms God's will, which stands behind the binding and the loosing. It is on the grounds of the gospel revelation that Christ is present with his church whenever two or three come together in his name to deal with these things. The priorities within the kingdom community, then, are this loving care of one another, a mutual encouragement to turn from everything that makes us stumble, and an unwillingness to compromise on truth or behaviour, because God has revealed to us from heaven, that which is bound in heaven and that which is loosed, in terms of the message of the kingdom.

Of course, that sort of living is not going to be easy. Peter speaks for us all when he asks Jesus to set some sort of limits on this matter of forgiveness. How about seven times, as the ceiling? (verse 21). I don't doubt that Peter had certain particular situations in mind. We know from his character in the Gospels how prone he was to open his mouth before his mind was in gear, and how often his impetuous words and behaviour landed him in trouble. But the implication here is that he is being outstandingly magnanimous, truly Christian, in fact. Whereas the rabbis taught the duty of forgiving three times, and no more, Peter raises the limit to seven. But, once again, Jesus' answer lifts the whole question on to an entirely different plane, re-interpreting all our normal human values. **'I tell you, not seven times, but seventy-seven times'** (verse 22). Many commentators point out that the reading '77' follows exactly the Greek of the Septuagint in Genesis 4:24, where Lamech declares that he will *avenge* himself seventy-seven times. This is probably a more accurate reading than 490, but the point is the same in either case. Who is going to keep track of that number of offences, or live long enough? Forgiveness must be the life-style of the Christian, a constant attitude, our reflex response. We are such sinners that we frequently hurt each other. That is why we need constantly to exercise and receive forgiveness towards one another. If we call Jesus 'Lord', we must do the Father's will and follow in the footsteps of the one who prayed, 'Father, forgive them,' even as he hung dying at the hands of wicked men. The parable that follows very powerfully sums up the teaching of this chapter.

> Therefore, the kingdom of heaven is like a king who wanted to settle accounts with his servants. As he began the settlement, a man who owed him ten thousand talents was brought to him. Since he was not able to pay, the master ordered that he and his wife and his children and all that he had be sold to repay the debt.
>
> The servant fell on his knees before him. 'Be patient with me,' he begged, 'and I will pay back everything.' The servant's master took pity on him, cancelled the debt and let him go.
>
> But when that servant went out, he found one of his fellow-servants who owed him a hundred denarii. He grabbed him and began to choke him. 'Pay back what you owe me!' he demanded.
>
> His fellow-servant fell to his knees and begged him, 'Be patient with me, and I will pay you back.'
>
> But he refused. Instead, he went off and had the man thrown into prison until he could pay the debt. When the other servants saw what had happened, they were greatly distressed and went and told their master everything that had happened.
>
> Then the master called the servant in. 'You wicked servant,' he said, 'I cancelled all that debt of yours because you begged me to. Shouldn't you have had mercy on your fellow-servant just as I had on you?' In anger his master turned him over to the jailers to be tortured, until he should pay back all he owed.
>
> 'This is how my heavenly Father will treat each of you unless you forgive your brother from your heart' (18:23-35).

The first servant's original debt is colossal. Ten thousand is the highest Greek numeral; the talent is the highest unit of currency. That is why it is described in verse 32 as '**all that debt of yours**'. By comparison, the other debt is trifling. Scholars have worked it out as a six hundred thousandth of the original. It is like the difference between an incalculable fortune and a 'fiver'. The first debt was so great it could never be repaid; the second is so petty it might easily have been overlooked.

But the forgiven servant is motivated by power over his debtor. He is going to make him sweat for every penny he owes. He can use violence against him and throw him into gaol, so he does. But he has made a fatal mistake. He has not understood the ground rules of the kingdom, for his actions deny everything Jesus has been teaching in this chapter. The kingdom of heaven is not about power but about love, not about law but grace, not about merit but mercy, not about getting but giving. It is not about status, but about being a little child, forgiving from the heart because we too have been forgiven. The world may say 'revenge is sweet', but Sir Walter Scott called it 'the sweetest morsel ever cooked in hell'. That is where it comes from and where it belongs.

The way of the new Israel is the way of free forgiveness from the heart, because the ultimate reality in all the universe is the character of the living God, whose heart is full of grace and love. Children of the kingdom are lovers of mercy. There are no alternative terms of membership. We have been freely forgiven all our debts; we must freely forgive one another, from our hearts (verse 35), or we do not take Jesus seriously.

10

Take the Medicine

The events of Matthew's Gospel are like a double row of pearls, threaded together on two strands which complement each other and unite all the different ingredients of the narrative together, as one whole. On the one strand are threaded many stories of fulfilment, where Jesus is revealed as the Messiah, received by faith, and where he gathers together a new community of believers who will constitute a replacement Israel, inheriting the promises made to Abraham. On the other strand, we discover stories of confrontation and increasing rejection as the breaking in of the kingdom in the claims of Christ the king move the narrative inexorably to the cross. Chapter 19 consists of three such incidents.

The Pharisees, with their test question on divorce (verses 1-12), and the rich, young ruler, with his dependence on his own ability to keep the law (verses 16-22) are both representative of a false confidence. They have missed the law's true purpose, which is to reveal the character of God and move us towards a deeper heart-likeness to him. But between these two dialogues, there is a short incident (verses 13-15) in which we are again reminded that little children are a picture of the citizens of the kingdom of heaven. It belongs to **such as these**, not to physical children, but to those who in childlike dependence believe in Christ and accept their new status as citizens of heaven's kingdom (e.g. 18:3-5).

The new Israel, then, consists of those who are 'little ones' in God's sight - **'Blessed are the poor in spirit, for theirs is the kingdom of heaven'** - and here in 19:27 those who have given up all to follow Christ. To them, **'I tell you the truth, at the renewal of all things, when the Son of Man sits on his glorious throne, you who have followed me will also sit on twelve thrones, judging the twelve tribes of Israel'** (verse 28). So the new community, represented by the disciples, will judge the old community. The followers of Jesus are given the privileges which those first offered them have rejected, by turning their backs on the king. This reversal theme, in 19:30, **'But many who are first will be last, and many who are last will be first'** is reiterated in 20:16, and illustrated in between, by the parable of the workers in the vineyard (20:1-15). The Pharisees have adopted totally erroneous views of the God of grace. They imagine that by their own activity and their own works they can actually make themselves acceptable to him. They would have no idea that God would be gracious to those 'called at the last hour', whether tax-collectors and sinners, any other Jewish outcasts, or indeed the Gentiles to whom the good news of the kingdom is beginning to spread.

But it is not only the Pharisees whose view of the kingdom is distorted. In chapter 20, we see that the thinking of the disciples still falls well short of the teaching they had. Mrs Zebedee comes to ask for the prize position for James and John (verses 20-23) but the other disciples' reaction of indignation and anger shows that their own thoughts were not so different. Jesus has to rebuke this Gentile attitude of wanting to lord it over others, with the sharp prohibition, **'Not so with you'** (verses 25-26a). Greatness in his kingdom will be measured by service and rulership experienced in slavery. That is the king's pattern.

At last, in chapter 21, the long journey up to Jerusalem ends, and the king rides in to his capital city, not as a conqueror on a war-horse, but **'gentle, and riding on a donkey'** (21:5), not **'to be served, but to serve, and to give his life as a ransom for many'** (20:28). He enters not only his city but his temple, which is its heart and soul. There, as he seeks to retrieve it to its proper use as a house of prayer, significantly, it is the 'little ones' who get their judgment about him right. The whole city is stirred by Christ's entry, in fulfilment of Zechariah 9:9, and asks, **'Who is this?'** (21:10). It is the children who are shouting in the temple area, **'Hosanna to the Son of David'** (21:15), and the chief priests and teachers of the law who are indignant and command Christ to silence them. There were plenty among the crowds ready to identify him simply as **Jesus, the prophet from Nazareth in Galilee** (21:11) but only the little ones really acknowledged his true identity and this was the fulfilment of the perfect praise predicted in Psalm 8:2. The quotation continues, 'because of your enemies, to silence the foe and the avenger.'

Even at this late stage in the Gospel, that central issue is still being debated. To the disciples, however, the meaning is made clear. First, there is the sign of the entry. This is followed by the sign of the cleansing of the temple, the sign in which the Lord suddenly comes to his temple, in fulfilment of Malachi 3:1. Finally, the incident regarding the fig-tree seems to sum up his actions of judgment on the Old Testament nation.

> Early in the morning, as he was on his way back to the city, he was hungry. Seeing a fig-tree by the road, he went up to it but found nothing on it except leaves. Then he said to it, 'May you never bear fruit again!' Immediately the tree withered (verses 18-19).

Reading that cold, as it were, it is hard for us to see the Old Testament precedents. Jeremiah 8:13 says, 'There will be no figs on the tree, and their leaves will wither. What I have given them will be taken from them,' a word of God in a judgment context. Or Micah 7:1, in the context of God calling to the city of Jerusalem, says, 'What misery is mine! ... there is no cluster of grapes to eat, none of the early figs that I crave.' So although Mark tells us that it was not yet time for figs, Jesus comes to a tree that is in early leaf, hoping to find early fruit and finds none. In picking up those Old Testament statements, this act clearly indicates that the temple with its barren religion and ritual is equally ripe for destruction; it has produced no fruit. And the rest of chapters 21 and 22 explore that theme with devastating consequences.

> Jesus entered the temple courts, and, while he was teaching, the chief priests and the elders of the people came to him. 'By what authority are you doing these things?' they asked. 'And who gave you this authority?'
>
> Jesus replied, 'I will also ask you one question. If you answer me, I will tell you by what authority I am doing these things. John's baptism - where did it come from? Was it from heaven, or from men?'
>
> They discussed it among themselves and said, 'If we say,

"From heaven," he will ask, "Then why didn't you believe him?"
But if we say, "From men" - we are afraid of the people, for they
all hold that John was a prophet.'
　So they answered Jesus, 'We don't know.'
　Then he said, 'Neither will I tell you by what authority I am
doing these things.'

'What do you think? There was a man who had two sons. He went
to the first and said, "Son, go and work today in the vineyard."
　' "I will not," he answered, but later he changed his mind and
went.
　'Then the father went to the other son and said the same thing.
He answered, "I will, sir," but he did not go.
　'Which of the two did what his father wanted?'
　'The first,' they answered.
　Jesus said to them, 'I tell you the truth, the tax collectors and
the prostitutes are entering the kingdom of God ahead of you. For
John came to you to show you the way of righteousness, and you
did not believe him, but the tax collectors and the prostitutes did.
And even after you saw this, you did not repent and believe him'
(Matthew 21:23-32).

In spite of the increasingly open hostility of the religious leaders,
Jesus returns the next day to the temple. It is *his* temple (as Malachi
had reminded the people) not *theirs*, and so the Lord of the temple uses
its courts for one of its great purposes - teaching the word of God. As
Matthew's account of the last week of Jesus' life moves towards its
climax, there is never a flicker of a doubt that he is in complete control
of all that is happening. We are never to imagine the Lord Jesus as a
helpless victim, swept away by an irresistible tide of human opposition. He is always the sovereign Lord, working out everything according to his Father's will, the master of every circumstance.
　Now, he faces the challenge of the opposition, and we are told by
Matthew that it centres in this double question, which the chief priests
and elders bring to him in verse 23: '**By what authority are you
doing these things? And who gave you this authority?**' That is
always the key question about who Jesus Christ is and what he does.
Every contemporary attack on the person of Jesus is actually asking

the question, What authority does this man have? Is he just an Essene community leader from Qumran, or is he the Son of God? Who gave him this authority? Was it just a crowd of people, who decided to follow him? Did he speak the word of the living God? Taking Jesus seriously is all about coming to terms with his authority.

For the Pharisees, the question revealed a genuine problem. Jesus had never been through the official rabbinic schools and yet he gathered more people in the temple to hear his teaching than any of the other religious authorities could possibly gather. Who does he think he is? That is still the central question of Christianity. In Pharisaical thinking, authority was a matter of status, based on paper qualifications. Many people still think in exactly the same way today. If you wanted to be a Pharisee, you went through the training. You passed the exams, or the equivalent, and you were qualified. You got your diploma, your degree and you were now a teacher of the law. That was fine. You had your status. But for Jesus, authority is a matter of service. The mighty works he did to relieve suffering, demonstrated God's love and authenticated God's power. They were justification in themselves of his authority, and every one of those mighty works is a statement of his identity and an implicit claim to deity.

So, when these religious leaders come to Jesus and question him about his authority, it is not because there is any shortage of evidence. He had demonstrated who he is over and over again. Those mighty acts are proof in themselves of his supernatural authority, and every one of them confirms his personal claims. No one else could heal as Jesus healed, or ever has done. No one else could feed five thousand people from one boy's lunch, or raise the dead with a word. No one else could still the storm. There is a uniqueness about the person of Jesus. That is why all the contemporary books, articles and TV programmes which attempt to destroy the divinity of Jesus by 're-interpreting' him for a modern audience always have to begin with a denial of the supernatural.

But if you take seriously the historical writings of the Gospels, and the teaching of the church, you see that from the very beginning the miracles of Jesus were an integral part of the story. Is it not significant that none of the first century opponents of Jesus denied that the miracles had happened? The attacks against Christianity by the Jewish rabbis of the later first century speak about him learning magic in Egypt, or claim that he was under occult powers. That much comes through the Gospel accounts too - 'he casts out demons by the prince of the demons' - but what they never said was that the miracles did not happen, because far too many people had seen them. There was no point in trying that line so early on. That had to wait for the nineteenth and twentieth centuries. In the first century, they had seen people raised, they were among the crowds who were fed, they knew he had done these things. But they had to find another explanation of who he was. He was continually exercising rights and authority that belong to God alone, yet they refused to believe that very plain message.

The problem with the Pharisees was not intellectual, but moral; not ignorance, but arrogance. They refused to accept the evidence that was set before their very eyes, because they were, in fact, rebels against the authority of God. That is always the root of the problem. It explains why our culture is so opposed to the real Jesus and why the shapers of its intellectual life and values in the arts and the media are so determined not to allow authentic, Biblical Christianity a hearing. The real Jesus is far too revolutionary and threatening for our secular culture to tolerate. He would blow it apart, just as he did the prevailing religious and nationalistic ethos of his own generation. The difference is that twentieth century culture wears the fashionable labels of atheism or agnosticism, while the first century opponents of Jesus seem to have genuinely believed their religion to be sincere and real. Perhaps, then, the closer parallel is in the lives of those who profess to believe in God and to be committed to the Christian faith. Why would we refuse the lordship of Jesus, if it is not because we do not want to submit to his authority in the details of our everyday lives?

Most of us human beings are quite bad at recognising ourselves; so in order to help the religious leaders understand what they were doing, Jesus raises with them a parallel issue, regarding the authority of another ministry than his own, the ministry of John the Baptist. By his gentle, probing, but totally demanding question, Jesus brings these men face to face with themselves, as they really are. He asks them to decide whether John's baptism came from heaven or from men, and in a moment he has exposed their hearts. These men had witnessed the multitudes of Jews who went out to John in the desert, when he was baptising in the Jordan. They had heard his calls to them to repent, and to symbolise this change of heart by being baptised, which was something that no Jew had ever needed to do. Baptism was reserved for Gentile proselytes who symbolised their acceptance of Judaism in that way. But above all, they had listened to John describe himself as the forerunner, and some may even have been there when he identified this man before them now, as 'the Lamb of God, who takes away the sin of the world' (John 1:29).

So Jesus challenges them: 'Was John mistaken or was he preaching the truth?' And of course, immediately they are trapped. Either they condemn themselves, as having refused the divine revelation, or they antagonise the crowds who had held John in great honour as a prophet.

I say that this exposes their hearts, because it shows, with great clarity, that they were not interested in the truth of the matter, but only in the expediency of what would be the better answer to keep their own reputation and influence intact. All they were concerned about was how the answer they gave would affect their status before men; whether they would be made to look fools, or to face hostility. The reality was that they had not believed in John any more than they believed in Jesus, because they didn't want to have to change their lives; but they would never admit that, openly. So they played games, or they tried to. They had to answer Jesus in that pathetically lame way, in verse 27, **'We don't know'**; and his reply is devastating, **'Neither will I tell you by what authority I am doing these things.'**

We misread that if we make it into a sort of 'tit for tat' response; it is far more serious than that. Jesus is saying that there is no point in him telling them that his authority is divine, because they will not face the reality of truth. They are not prepared to deal with the facts, only opinions and blind prejudice, so God will leave them to their silly games. Their stubborn unbelief will produce its own fruit of increasing ignorance.

'Leave them, they are blind guides [of the blind],' Jesus told his disciples earlier (15:14), but before he does that here, he appeals to the Pharisees to think again, through the parable of the two sons. **'What do you think?'** he says, and I love that question, because even at this late stage in his ministry, just days away from the cross, Jesus is still pleading with the Pharisees to use their minds, to think. Christianity is never irrational, though revelation may lead us beyond human reason. We have everything to gain if we can persuade our generation to think, seriously and consistently, about the claims of Jesus Christ. Our culture may imagine that it needs a 'bendy' Jesus, malleable, flexible, ready to take on whatever shape they want him to be, but that can only be so at the expense of the historical Jesus, the only real Jesus there is. That Jesus never encouraged mere abstract, intellectual speculation about spiritual things; he knew how arid and unproductive that would be. But neither did he ever by-pass the mind.

If people are going to grasp the truth of who Jesus Christ is, it has to go through the mind to the heart, in order to activate the will. You can never bypass the mind. That is why in the Acts of the Apostles, as the gospel was spreading throughout the whole world of that day, we find it spread in terms of understanding, reasoning, persuading, discussing, and proclaiming. They are all words that affect the mind. And Jesus is here appealing to the Pharisees to use their minds.

We are often told that the parables of Jesus are marvellously good stories as indeed they are; but they are designed not just to entertain us, but to activate our minds. That important principle is taught in Paul's second letter to Timothy, where he writes, 'Think over what I say and the Lord will give you understanding' (2 Timothy 2:7). The two things go together. If you do the thinking, God will give you the understanding. If you put your mind under the authority of the word of God, he will grant you insight. We tend to think that he ought to give us the understanding - without us needing to think. That is a reflection of our passive spirituality, where we think God should do all our thinking for us and present us with all the answers about every question, instantly, served up on a plate. But it is the exercise of the mind in the truth of God that produces conviction and solid faith. There is no instant substitute for that and without it unbelief will harden into ignorance, as it did with the Pharisees. The parable makes this very point.

Both boys are told by their father to serve him that working day in the vineyard. The first refuses, but afterwards changes the mind. He repents and goes. Initially his refusal is very blunt and even defiantly rebellious - **'I will not,' he answered** (verse 29). But eventually he demonstrates a real repentance in his action. By contrast, the second son seems incredibly eager. In his response, all the emphasis is on the 'I', **'I will, sir,' but he did not go** (verse 30). There seems to be a deliberate self-contrast here with his unwilling brother. He claims to be so much better, because he will obey his father instantly and fully, but he does nothing. We don't know if he ever intended to go; we are not told that, because it is actions, not intentions, about which Jesus was concerned. There comes the inevitable question. **'Which of the two did what his father wanted?'** And even the Pharisees can't get that one wrong. **'The first, they answered.'**

But then we hear the devastating application of that, which Jesus makes. **'I tell you the truth,'** he says, **'the tax collectors and prostitutes are entering the kingdom of God ahead of you'** (verse 31). He takes them right back to the issue they thought they had dodged. He had asked them about John's mission and John's authority, and they had said they did not know. But the people whom one might have assumed to be the least likely to know apparently did, and acted on what they had discovered. There were the tax-collectors (condemned by the religious leaders as traitors to God and his people because of their collaboration with the Romans), and the prostitutes (condemned because of their gross immorality). Both, because of their greed, had been living lives which loudly and defiantly said to God, 'I will not.' But when they heard John's preaching of the way of righteousness, they were prepared to listen, to think it through, to change their minds and follow with their actions, because they believed the word of God from his lips.

But what of the religious leaders? Here were the people who professed allegiance to God, and who called themselves his servants. But when he calls them to repent of their religious sins, their love of position and pride and to put his service first, they are full of words, but without any actions. Christ has come into the world to do the heavenly Father's will. But these people are not really interested in doing his will at all. Their religion was serving themselves, for their own purposes and their own status.

Jesus comes to the world as the model Son and the ideal Servant. As Hebrews 10:5-7, expresses it, '... when Christ came into the world, he said ... "Here I am ... I have come to do your will, O God."' He came to fulfil the will of the Father perfectly in keeping the law in its totality, as no other man ever had done, or could do. He fulfilled the ideal of the law, in the pattern of a human life lived in perfect obedience to the will of God, and he brought that to its completion by fulfilling all the Father's purposes, even to death on the cross.

But those who professed to be God's earthly representatives were actually doing the very opposite, rejecting his commands and denying his authority. So, the tables are turned. The despised are accepting God's call, while those first called are avoiding his heart requirements and revealing themselves to be cold and loveless, proud and prejudiced. Moreover, even though Jesus has pointed this out to them, they still did not repent and believe. Even though they saw the changes God had made in the lives of those who responded to John's message, they still hardened their hearts.

It should not surprise us to see those same symptoms in some of today's Christian leadership, though it will grieve us. If we are prepared to listen, to think and to take Jesus seriously we may find such symptoms in our own hearts, also.

11

Hear the Verdict

Chapters 21-23 of Matthew, which immediately precede the last great discourse of Jesus in this Gospel, focus almost exclusively on his conflict with the religious leaders in Jerusalem. There are at least two reasons for this. Firstly, the cross is the climax of the Gospel and therefore requires a full explanation of why it happened and what it signifies. But also, the new community, which Christ's death on the cross will make possible, is increasingly clearly defined and understood by contrast with the old order which is passing away. That is implicit in Christ's warning to the chief priests and elders that the tax collectors and prostitutes were entering the kingdom of God ahead of them (21:31). There is a growing sense of urgency about Christ's teaching, as the remaining time of his earthly ministry diminishes, not because there is any incompleteness in his work, but because time is running out for the old Israel.

The kingdom changed

In the parable of the tenants (21:33-44), Jesus confronts the leaders with their neglect of their covenant obligations, indeed with their actual antagonism towards the work which God is doing. Down the generations their forefathers had rejected and killed the messengers God sent them, and now they are about to do away with the Son and heir. This meaning was not lost on the Pharisees (verse 45), nor was the picture overdrawn, for when they had heard the parable they went off to plot Jesus' arrest (verse 46).

But the most important ingredient of the parable is the solemn statement Jesus makes, as the confrontation theme comes to its peak. **'Therefore I tell you that the kingdom of God will be taken away from you and given to a people who will produce its fruit'** (verse 43) - echoes of the fig tree; **'He who falls on this stone will be broken to pieces.'** There is the humbling, 'the little children' idea, of coming into the kingdom; **'but he on whom it falls will be crushed'** - there is the idea of judgment and utter destruction.

These parables are making increasingly clear the fact that the old order has gone. Unless they acknowledge Christ as the king and turn to him, in repentance and faith, there is no hope left for Israel. The same note is sounded again in the parable of the wedding banquet (22:1-14) where all the gracious initiatives and invitations of the king are treated with churlish contempt and rejection: **'The king was enraged. He sent his army and destroyed those murderers and burned their city'** (verse 7). As a result the invitation to his son's wedding banquet goes out to anyone who will accept it, but the standards that the king requires still pertain, even in this changed situation. At the end of the parable comes the incident where one of the newly invited guests thinks he can appear inappropriately dressed, 'without wedding clothes'. As a result, he is thrown out of the feast, warning us that acceptance of the free invitation does not make us immune from living the kingdom life-style. Dr. Dick France's comment is very helpful here. He writes, 'It was the claim to belong to the kingdom without an appropriate change of life which characterised the old Israel, and brought about its rejection. The new people of God must not fall into the same error.' The extension of the kingdom does not dilute the king's requirements in his people.

The rest of chapter 22 is a series of controversies or questions, all valid in their way, but all part of the general conspiracy to try **to trap him in his words** (verse 15). In verses 15-22, it is the Pharisees with their catch question about paying taxes to Caesar, followed by the Sadducees, in verses 23-32, with their ludicrous question about marriage and the resurrection. The cynicism of this is plain when Matthew tells us that they did not even believe in the resurrection. In verses 34-40, it is the expert in the law with his fast ball on the middle stump, **'Teacher, which is the greatest commandment in the Law?'** The fulfilment and confrontation are moving closer together as we come to the end of the chapter, and then Jesus suddenly turns the tables on his interrogators with the ultimate challenge to them, in the form of the one essential, basic question (verse 42): **'What do you think about the Christ? Whose son is he?'** When they give the orthodox reply, **'The son of David,'** Jesus poses a further question.

'How is it then that David, speaking by the Spirit, calls him "Lord"?' That is the real battle issue, which has been developing all through the Gospel. If Christ demonstrates all that was prophesied about the Messiah, if he is 'great David's greater Son', and all the evidence points to that reality, then will he be accepted as Lord? The Christ is more than a great prophet, or leader, or even king. He is not just David's son, he is David's Lord. And as Jesus makes that declaration from Psalm 110, probably the greatest Messianic psalm, the debate is over. **No-one could say a word in reply, and from that day on no-one dared to ask him any more questions** (verse 46). In the end, we either fall at his feet and crown him as our king, or we walk away, disinterested.

In chapter 23, we listen to the judge pronouncing the verdict. The debating is over; the trial is finished. But the one they thought of as their prisoner, and who in a few days will literally fulfil that role, first declares himself to be the judge and finds his accusers guilty on all counts. He displays the evidence on which his righteous judgment will be based. To the crowds gathered in the temple, and to his disciples, Jesus says, **'The teachers of the law and the Pharisees sit in Moses' seat. So you must obey them and do everything they tell you. But do not do what they do, for they do not practise what they preach'** (verses 2, 3). There is the devastating indictment. Can you think of a more appalling condemnation than that? **'... they do not practise what they preach.'** They are hypocrites, as he is going to call them over and over again in this chapter, and the reason for that, is that **everything they do is done for men to see** (verse 5).

Jesus did not object to their calling or to their teaching, in so far as it was true to the law of Moses rather than the traditions of the elders. It was their behaviour that grieved and appalled him. They had become posers, performers on a stage, as unlike what they pretended to be in 'real life', as actors wearing masks were unlike the characters they portrayed in the Greek drama. These were the literal 'hypocrites', who wore large mechanical masks, with fixed stereotyped expressions, and containing devices for augmenting their voices. They were not themselves, and neither were the Pharisees what their public image suggested. This is the great danger of all religious practice. Whenever we agree to the truth and fail to live by it;

whenever our motivation is what other people will see and how they will think of us; whenever we put on a mask and refuse to be real about ourselves, then however much we may profess that we want to please God, we have become blind to the fact that he calls our 'Let's pretend to be Christians', hypocrisy.

That is the old Judaism, the old Israel, arraigned by the king, who has come to his temple, suddenly, as Malachi said he would, and who finds no fruit, nothing that brings him joy, nothing that is the fulfilment of his promises. The Pharisees have been so consumed by the externals - the robes that they wear, the phylacteries, the tassels of their prayer-shawls, the places of honour at the banquets, the important seats in the synagogue, the title of rabbi - all externals. But the greatest of all tragedies is that they were blissfully unaware of it. Though they were 'play actors', we are not to derive from that the idea that they were deliberate shams, or consciously insincere. They were actually self-deceived, 'blind guides', as Jesus called them. They were so much men of this world that they did not even realise, nor could they, how displeasing the system they had constructed was to God.

Leaders in the kingdom

Verses 8-12 are in some ways the most important in the whole chapter for they provide a positive corrective for the disciples, and for us.

> **But you are not to be called 'Rabbi', for you have only one Master and you are all brothers. And do not call anyone on earth 'father', for you have one Father, and he is in heaven. Nor are you to be called 'teacher', for you have one Teacher, the Christ. The greatest among you will be your servant. For whoever exalts himself will be humbled, and whoever humbles himself will be exalted.**

We must take these prohibitions seriously. Christian leaders are not to be known by titles or descriptions of their office, which are designed to mark them off from lesser mortals or to rank them alongside equivalent figures in other professions, or even religions. The root reason is the different principle of authority which applies in the new covenant community. Judaism was torn apart by arguments over minutiae of practice between different rabbis and their supporters, and still is. The result is that there is no clear, authentic voice. That was why Jesus' teaching was so different from that of the scribes. We have one Master, one supreme authority, Jesus Christ, who is the truth and before whom we are all equal, all brothers. There is no room for a hierarchy of teaching authority in Christ's church. It is in that teaching context that the term 'father' is prohibited, because again it implies a superiority which is inappropriate in the family of God, when we are all equally children of our one Father, who is in heaven. Our one teacher is the Christ, the only ultimate authority, in heaven and on earth, so no human instructor is to arrogate that title to himself.

But that is precisely what we do! In many denominations, church titles abound - reverend, very reverend, most reverend, right reverend. Even in churches which avoid such additions, the title 'pastor' is often used. Ministers pursue degrees and diplomas, wear academic gowns and hoods and religious vestments which mark them out as superior to others. In some countries, it is now impossible to be appointed as a pastor-teacher in a congregation without a doctorate. This has led to a scramble for practical Doctor of Ministry qualifications and programmes, leading to what David Wells of Gordon-Conwell Seminary has dubbed 'the D-min-ization of the ministry'.

We cannot, of course, judge the motivation of others' hearts, but are not these common practices both a great snare to most of us, in our human sinfulness and pride, and a great distraction from the principles of ministry which Jesus envisaged for his disciples? **'The greatest among you will be your servant'** (verse 11). Is that really what we look for as the model of ministry in the contemporary church? I do not think so. Leon Morris comments, 'Throughout his teaching Jesus insists that his followers must be lowly. He set the example himself, for in his whole life he forsook the corridors of power and was content to be a lowly teacher, mostly in the remote rural areas of the province in which he lived.' That is a long way from our contemporary ministerial career ladders, our denominational hierarchies and our status-conscious congregations. But there is a price to pay, **'for whoever exalts himself will be humbled'** and the decline of the church in the western world may well be due in no small measure to the fact that many of its adherents have never really taken Jesus seriously in this and in many other practical areas.

Israel condemned

At verse 13, Jesus launches into seven woes, or pronouncements of judgment, which take up most of the rest of the chapter. They constitute the king's indictment against his faithless people. Strongly Jewish in both theme and content, it is perhaps appropriate that the structure of this passage should follow a pattern called *chiasm*, which is very prevalent in the Old Testament, being typically Hebrew. The seven woes are arranged so that the first and last numbers, 2 and 6, 3 and 5, balance one another, the focus being then on the middle ingredient of the pattern (the fourth woe) where the major point is made. This follows the text of the NIV where verse 14 is omitted, as it is from the best manuscripts.

The first and seventh woes deal with Israel's refusal to accept God's messengers and therefore to receive and respond to his word. In their opposition to Christ and his word, throughout his ministry, they have not only shut this door of the kingdom on themselves, but have taught others who listen to them to reject it too (verse 13). Balanced with this is the seventh woe, where, like their ancestors, the religious leaders are happy to honour dead heroes by building decorative tombs for the prophets whom their fathers murdered, but will not receive God's word from his living messengers, and especially from Christ himself. Thus, they prove to be true sons of their rebellious fathers (verses 29-32).

The second and sixth woes focus on the misdirected religious zeal of the hypocrites, which, far from serving God's purposes, does more harm than good. What is the point of travelling over sea and land to make proselytes, if all you are converting them to is to be **twice as much a son of hell**? (verse 15). Outward religiosity, covering a heart of hypocrisy and wickedness, is no better than a whitewashed tomb, made acceptable outwardly, but inwardly full of decay and bones.

The third and fifth woes expose the distortion of the Scriptures which the hypocrites practised by their addition. Verses 16-22 are an extended indictment about the swearing of oaths, in which the nice distinction made about whether an oath sworn by the gold of the temple is more binding than one sworn on the temple alone, because the one is more valuable than the other, is blown sky-high. This is balanced by a woe dealing with ritual washings (verses 25, 26), where preoccupation with the outside can all too often lead to neglect of inner cleansing. In both cases, the purpose or spirit of the law has been distorted, or even lost, by adding to its letter. This is the familiar theme that by adding their own codicils, restrictions and additions, the hypocrites domesticated God's law, bringing it down to a manageable size which they could cope with and control.

The fourth and central woe, which following the chiasmic pattern is the major point that is to be made, deals firstly with tithing, but swiftly moves on to the foundational indictment: **'Woe to you teachers of the law and Pharisees, you hypocrites! You give a tenth of your spices – mint, dill and cummin. But you have neglected the more important matters of the law** (and here is the heart of it) – **justice, mercy and faithfulness. You should have practised the latter without neglecting the former. You blind guides! You strain out a gnat, but swallow a camel'** (verses 23, 24). In the end, it was what the Pharisees did not do which revealed their true heart. In their myopic obsession with the details of their man-made rules and regulations, they missed the great qualities of the character of its Giver, which the law reveals and requires in the lives of those who receive it. On the matters of justice, mercy and faithfulness, they are weighed in the balance and found wanting.

There can be only one verdict, and it is pronounced in verses 37-39, not with any sort of vindictiveness, but in great compassion and heart-felt grief:

> **'O Jerusalem, Jerusalem, you who kill the prophets and stone those sent to you, how often I have longed to gather your children together, as a hen gathers her chicks under her wings, but you were not willing. Look, your house is left to you desolate. For I tell you, you will not see me again until you say, "Blessed is he who comes in the name of the Lord."'**

Having refused the protection that could be hers only by submission to the authority of her covenant Lord, Jerusalem is left desolate, empty because abandoned by God. He is leaving them. He will not be found any more in the temple. The outward forms and ceremonies may continue for another forty years or so, until the invading legions of Rome will eventually destroy both city and temple in 70 AD. But the sentence is pronounced now. What is true of the temple is true of the city and of the nation - God will no longer dwell with a people who stubbornly and persistently refuse to honour him.

The immediate fulfilment of the verse follows in 24:1: **Jesus left the temple and was walking away ... .** He never returned; but he will, when he comes in judgment at the parousia. When the king returns in the manifestation of his power and glory, at the end of time, then all the world (even the resistant populace of Jerusalem) will stand before his throne and recognise him as the 'one who comes in the name of the Lord'. But now, just as Ezekiel had seen the throne of God remove from Jerusalem at the time of the exile, so the disciples watch, as the true occupant of that throne, their rejected king, leaves the temple, the city and the nation, as he prepares to accomplish his Exodus, and with it bring about the formation of a new covenant community, a new Israel.

Relevant for today
As always, in this study, we need to understand the historical context of the passages we are considering, in order to grasp as fully as we can the impact these words would have had both on the original hearers and on Matthew's original readers. We have to understand what it meant *then*, in order rightly to apply it to *now*. But that journey of application must be made. The danger with much of our Bible study is that we want to make it too quickly. We seize on the nearest points of similarity between their situation and ours, or we project our needs and problems on to the Biblical account, as though the account was written specifically to us in the particularity of our twentieth century situation. We are not the Pharisees; two thousand years separate us from them and inevitably some of the nuances of the situation are hidden from us in the mists of time. But we are sinful human beings, and we shall find in our hearts the same seeds of stubborn rebellion against God which Jesus detected and exposed in theirs. As Paul said, about the Old Testament, 'Everything that was written in the past was written to teach us, so that through endurance and the encouragement of the Scriptures we might have hope' (Romans 15:4). It is just as true when we study these Gospel narratives. We are not dealing with

antiquities, but with the burning issues of our own hearts, before God.

In summary, then, what are we as late twentieth-century Christians to make of these devastating indictments and attacks on first-century Judaism, from the lips of Jesus? Once the details of cultural circumstances, such as tithing mint, dill and cummin, are removed, we see an exposure of the works-religion that is endemic to the human race whenever we want to put ourselves in the right with God. Look at all the religions of the world and you will discover a variety of methods, ladders to climb, by which human beings can make themselves acceptable to whatever god or gods they believe in. Christianity stands alone as the only world faith to say that there is no ladder by which we can climb to God, no amount of good works or religious devotion that can atone for our sin or make us acceptable to a holy, just and sovereign God. The glory of the gospel of the kingdom is that God has come down the ladder to us, to rescue us when we were powerless to help ourselves and to lavish on us his free mercy when we deserve only his wrath and punishment. Our response can only be, 'Nothing in my hand I bring, simply to thy cross I cling.' That is the very opposite of all that comes naturally to men and women in our fallen, sinful state. We want to excuse ourselves, to blame others, to get ourselves out of the predicament we are in - anything rather than come humbly, repentantly to God and receive his forgiveness as a free gift. That was the problem with the Pharisees too.

Once our eyes are off God and the way he says things are to be done, our spiritual vision is prone to all sorts of distortion without us even realizing it. The problem of the Pharisees was that of inverted values. The things they stressed as important and prided themselves in, God rejected. The concerns of his heart (justice, mercy, faithfulness) did not find a place on their agenda. But it never occurred to them, beyond perhaps the moment when Jesus' penetrating words first hit home, that they could be wrong. They judged everything from the standpoint they had chosen to adopt as though that were the ultimate reality. I am reminded of a little girl who when she got her first pair of glasses, said, 'I always thought everybody saw things fuzzy like that.' Or what about the older person, going deaf, who complains that the trouble with all the young people today is that they mutter and mumble? In spiritual matters, the Pharisees warn us to check ourselves carefully when we start from the premise, 'I must be right.' Indeed, we are to recognise that we shall rarely express things that baldly. We are much more likely to introduce our distorted views with a phrase like, 'I may be wrong, but...' which usually means 'I am sure that I am right'!

We are suffering from distorted vision when human rules and regulations become more important to us than divine priorities. So scrupulous were the Pharisees about tithing that they even extended it to the small aromatic herbs grown to flavour their food. There was nothing in the law of Moses about this. It stresses only tithing the three main crops - grain, wine and oil. But it is not so difficult to appreciate the attraction to the Pharisees of such meticulous detailed attention to such minor matters. 'Faithfulness in little things is a very great thing,' we are told. What a faithful, committed man he must be to weigh out the mint he picks in the garden, to put in the peas, and then devote a tenth of it to the temple. Our natural works-religion assures us that this must be pleasing to God. Surely, it will secure his blessing.

However, that is not the religion of the Bible at all. It is not 'What a good boy am I!', but 'God, be merciful to me, the sinner.' The further danger of course is that such man-centred legalism hardens the heart towards others. If I think I am making my number with God by hard work, keeping all the sub-cultural rules of my Christian group, I am not going to be very understanding of other people's failures. If God makes these heavy demands on me, why should I let other people off any more lightly? So the real requirements of the law are overlooked. 'He has showed you, O man, what is good. And what does the LORD require of you? To act justly and to love mercy and to walk humbly with your God' (Micah 6:8). It's not about weighing out herbs at all! Tithing was a part of the Old Testament law, which Jesus said should not be neglected; but the absurd lengths to which the Pharisees had taken things provided a screen behind which they could hide themselves from the real demands of the law's penetrating requirements.

'How often have I longed ... but you were not willing' (verse 37). There are no sadder words from Christ's lips in the whole Gospel. The will is at the heart of things because God has created us as responsible human beings and he will hold us to account for our actions. It is not that we have a free will, because we are born sinners, with a will that is already biased away from God. But we are responsible and we do make choices, which have long-lasting effects in our lives. Moreover, we are not left without direction or authority. We do not live in a moral maze, where we cannot be certain of the outcome of the decisions we make. God has spoken into our world and his word is truth. That was the heart of Old Testament religion, which the Pharisees seemed to have forgotten.

What marked Israel out from the pagan nations all around her, with their dumb, blind, deaf, inert idols, was that she worshipped the living God who spoke, and saw, and heard and acted, the God who 'came down to deliver'. The pagan 'deities' could be numbered by their thousands, but Israel was taught, 'The LORD our God, the LORD is one' (Deuteronomy 6:4). The pagans identified their gods with the forces of nature, but Israel worshipped a transcendent Creator who was separate from everything he had made (and he had made everything). The pagans' religion was therefore an extension of their own experience, a coming to terms with the unexplained realities of life in the world, but Israel received a revelation from outside the world of experience in the word of the living God, who spoke and it was done. Her religion was not a human projection, but a divine disclosure.

The God who had brought everything into being explained the meaning of his world and the purposes of his sovereign will. The pagans had no sense of absolute morality, whereas Israel had the Lord's commandments, a knowledge of right and wrong based on the character of God. The pagans thought of history as a circle, the passage of the year, the cycle of birth to death to decay to new birth. Israel saw history as a linear progression, from the creation to the end of all things in the coming of the kingdom of God, and through it all God was in control, working his purposes out. To move from this great anchor point back to the world of self-determination, to rewrite the rules as the Pharisees did, was a means of coming to terms with the natural world of human sinfulness and a move back towards the accommodation of Old Testament idolatry. Their hypocrisy was to turn the living God into a pocket-sized deity, whom they could control and manipulate by their mechanized rule-keeping. Their ultimate authority lay within themselves, rather than with God.

That must always happen when we nullify the word of God. As

we apply the lessons of these chapters to our very different cultural context, that, at least, remains clear. We are at our most vulnerable spiritually when we stop listening carefully to the word of God, in Scripture. A modern application has been made very powerfully by David Wells in his book *No Place for Truth*, subtitled 'Whatever happened to Evangelical Theology?' He writes:

'Where is the focus of God's truth to be found? To the pagan who heard the voice of the gods within, who listened to the whisperings of intuition, and to the modern who similarly listens within for the voice of self, the answer is the same. For the Israelite it was different. The Bible is not a remarkable illustration of what we have already heard within ourselves; it is a remarkable discovery of what we have not and cannot hear within ourselves ... It is how we apply ourselves to learn what God has disclosed of himself in a realm outside ourselves that is important. And unless we steadfastly maintain this distinction in the face of the modern pressures to destroy it, we will soon find that we are using the Bible merely to corroborate the validity of what we have already found within our religious consciousness - which is another way of saying that we are putting ourselves in place of the Bible. It is another way of reasserting the old paganism. When that happens, theology is irredeemably reduced to autobiography, and preaching degenerates into mere story telling.

The bottom line for our modernized world is that there is no truth; the bottom line for Christian consciousness is precisely the opposite. The Christian predisposition to believe in the kind of truth that is objective and public and that reflects ultimate reality cuts across the grain of what modernity considers plausible.[6]

Paganism, Pharisaism, modernity - they all have this much in common: they nullify the word of God, and at the end of the day their house is left desolate. We do well to take Jesus seriously.

12

Anticipate the Coming

We come now to the final unit of teaching, the fifth discourse in Matthew's Gospel. It begins, as the first unit did, with Jesus seated as a rabbi, on a hillside, instructing the disciples (24:3 echoes 5:1-2). It ends with a version of the familiar formula Matthew uses, '**When Jesus had finished saying all these things ...**' (26:1). But not only do the structural marker-points clearly delineate chapters 24 and 25 as a single discourse, the content confirms it as Jesus proceeds to give a very detailed answer to a highly specific question. Having pronounced sentence on the old Israel as he leaves the temple for the very last time, Jesus prophesies, '**not one stone here will be left on another; every one will be thrown down**' (24:2). The question, which is actually in two parts, as the following answer clearly is, follows in verse 3: '**Tell us, when will this happen, and what will be the sign of your coming and of the end of the age?**' They move on, out of the city, to the Mount of Olives as the most suitable spot, with its view over the whole city, for Jesus to answer the disciples' questions as he sets the pattern for the church's eschatology. For the whole thrust of his answer is to teach the disciples how to be living *now*, in the limited fulfilment of the kingdom, which is the experience of the church on earth, but always in the perspective of the *not yet*, when the Son of man will come in the clouds, **with power and great glory** (verse 30). Like them, we too are to live these days in the light of that great day. The pronouncement of judgment on the old Israel is followed immediately by the private instruction of the new.

The key to understanding chapter 24 is the nature of the disciples' question in verse 3. They are linked together as one event or sequence of events, the destruction of the temple (which Jesus prophesied in verse 2), the sign of his parousia, and the end of the age. Jesus has already taught them, in chapter 13, about the separation of the wheat and the weeds at the end of the age. In chapter 28, he will promise his presence constantly with his evangelising church up to the end of the age. The disciples knew that event would be the coming of the kingdom in judgment, so not unnaturally, they took the destruction of the temple and the second coming of Jesus, and put them together, as one package. But Jesus' answer clearly separates out what we might call the near horizon of AD 70, from the far horizon of his second coming. The fall of Jerusalem was the completion of the close of the Jewish era, the fulfilment of the woes that he had pronounced, which began with that generation's rejection of their Messiah. But the last judgment will be the close of the human era. By recognising that chapters 24 and 25 form one unit, it becomes clear that the two horizons, the destruction of Jerusalem and the second coming of Jesus, are in view throughout the discourse.

However, a further complication for the interpreter is that the language used is partly literal and partly symbolic, and it is not always easy to distinguish which is which. In one sense, the disciples were quite right to bracket the two horizons together, although Jesus wants them to grasp that the events will not be contemporaneous, or even in an immediate chronological sequence. Still, the earlier events, in the fall of Jerusalem, are a foreshadowing or representative type of the climactic end of all things. Jesus, as the prophet, par excellence, is here fulfilling another of the predicted Old Testament roles of Messiah, and as such he uses a very common Old Testament prophetic methodology. This is usually called *prophetic foreshortening*, the idea being that events in the near future and those much further ahead, are spoken of as if they are very close together, because they have common characteristics. We can understand this in terms of looking at a mountain range. From a distance, mountains which may be very many miles apart seem to be close together; but as you get nearer to them, so your perspective changes and you begin to see the real distances which separates peak from peak. That is what often happens in Old Testament prophecy. Take, for example, the classic example of Isaiah. He sees the destruction of Babylon and the final day of the Lord as if it was one day of divine judgment. The same pattern emerges in both but we now know that there are many centuries between those two events, that the two peaks, as it were, have a huge distance separating them. But because of their similarities, they are both called 'the day of the Lord' in the closing chapters of Isaiah's prophecy.

God's final judgment, then, will be the culmination of his many acts of judgment, which will have preceded it. In fact Paul tells the Romans that this judgment is always active in God's governorship of the world, for 'the wrath of God is being revealed from heaven against all the godlessness and wickedness of men who suppress the truth' (Romans 1:18). Similarly, the fall of Jerusalem is a picture of the end of the age, for in both, God the king comes to judge.

One further important indication of this, for the interpreter, is that a prophet often speaks about large-scale events, cosmic events even, which have eternal repercussions, but he sets them in the cultural context of his own time and within his own geographical horizons. Whenever we come to interpret Biblical prophecy we always have to begin with what this meant in that situation, to those people who first heard it. It was the relevant word of God to them in their context. This helps to guard us against the often popular, but fanciful, interpretations of prophecies into the specific details of our own contemporary context. So, any interpretation of the prophecy of Ezekiel, for example, which requires the interpreter to have a contemporary knowledge of the movements of the American Sixth Fleet in the Mediterranean, is always going to be suspect! It could not have meant that to the people who heard Ezekiel deliver those words. First of all, we must look at what it meant in their setting, their own cultural, geographical background. Then, beyond that, we shall often find a fulfilment in the person of Jesus, within his work and his ministry, and beyond that, at another level, in the return of Christ at the end of time, when he comes as king and judge. So what is painted in Jewish and Palestinian colours does not apply to those contexts; it may well have a wider framework of reference.

Signs of the end

Matthew 24 is a long and complex chapter. By general agreement, it is not an easy one for any interpreter to deal with. However, I hope it will help us to find our way through, if we keep in mind that Jesus identifies three major signs, or characteristics, which answer the disciples' initial request.

At the basic level in this chapter, we are looking at signs that are characteristic of 'the last days', which, Biblically, are the days between the first and the second comings. Obviously, within the last days there will be the last, last days, which one generation will live through, but 'the last days' refers to that whole period, which some people call the church age or the age of salvation, the age between the ascension of Christ and his return in glory.

The first is the sign of *distress*. Older versions translate this Greek word *thlipsis* as 'tribulation'. It occurs three times in the passage. It is obscured, in the NIV, when it first occurs at verse 9: **'Then you will be handed over to be persecuted.'** The verbal phrase *to be persecuted* represents this noun, *distress* or *tribulation*. It occurs again in verse 21, **'For then there will be great distress, great tribulation unequalled from the beginning of the world until now.'** Thirdly, it is used in verse 29, **'Immediately after the distress of those days'**.

So the paragraph beginning in verse 9, which starts with predictions very similar to the warnings of persecution in Matthew 10, and which could easily refer to the immediate post-apostolic church, ends in verse 14 with the worldwide preaching of the gospel. **'Then you will be handed over to be persecuted and put to death; and you will be hated by all nations because of me'** (verse 9). Distress here signifies persecution, and the early church could very easily see themselves in that fulfilment. There were those who, under that pressure, turned away from the faith, otherwise the letter to the Hebrews would not have needed to be written. There were many false prophets who invaded the church and deceived many people. The love of many undoubtedly grew cold (verses 10-12). But we cannot just restrict this to the early church, because in verse 14, Jesus speaks about this gospel of the kingdom being preached in the whole world, **'and then the end will come'**.

I am writing this manuscript, using a new pair of spectacles which have graded lenses. Instead of bifocals where you have two distinct and separate lenses with different focal lengths, the varying lens gradually merges from one to the other. That is what is happening in this chapter. We tend to want to see things with the distinction of a bifocal approach - this is AD 70, this is the second coming. But much of what Jesus says applies to the whole period before his return, as the gospel has gone out into all the world. Clearly that prediction is not limited to AD 70, but it will have been fulfilled by the time he comes again.

However, from verse 15, there is a paragraph which is clearly of specific reference to the fall of Jerusalem. Indeed, many commentators point out that by following Jesus' instructions to the letter, the Christian community fled the city, when they saw the Roman legions surrounding Jerusalem before AD 70, and saved their lives by putting into practice what they were being told here. This has led some to suggest that Jesus' teaching actually divides neatly into two. On this view there are perspectives here about the far future, but really verses 4-28 are all about the events leading up to and climaxing in the rejection of the Jews and the destruction of the city and temple in AD 70. That certainly works well for the paragraph from verse 15 to verse 21.

But if the following verses up to 28 are all about AD 70, why does verse 29 begin, **'Immediately after the distress of those days the sun will be darkened and the moon will not give its light ... At that time the sign of the Son of Man will appear in the sky ...'** and go on to talk about the second coming? It is very attractive to have the bifocal approach; it makes this chapter a lot easier. Verses 4-28 refer to 70 AD, all the rest after that to the second coming. But the word 'immediately' in verse 29 is a major difficulty. For here we are, over 1900 years later, still awaiting his appearing!

If it is simply that the first part of the chapter refers to Jerusalem, then this division of the material must indicate that Jesus was mistaken in saying he would come **'immediately after the distress of those days'**. That of course is the standard liberal, critical view. He expected his coming to be immediate, but he was wrong and all attempts to get round that view will fail unless we take both the 'now' and the 'not-yet' views together. Some of this refers to Jerusalem in A.D. 70 and some of it refers to the second coming, and we, of course are in a better position to see that than the disciples were as they listened to Jesus speaking. On this reading then, distress or tribulation is characteristic of the entire last days period, but it would appear to be particularly intense immediately before the return of the Lord Jesus. The great distress immediately before his return in verse 29 is paralleled in verse 21 by a distress **unequalled from the beginning of the world until now**.

The second sign is the sign of *apostasy*, mentioned in verses 10-12 and verse 24. Again, it is clear that this sign is associated with both events. In the letter to the Hebrews, 2 Peter, 1 John and in the Pastoral epistles, we are taught that apostasy is characteristic of the whole period; it is a mark of 'the last days'. But if we turn for a moment to what Paul has to teach about this in 2 Thessalonians 2:1-3, we discover that it will be particularly intense before the return of Christ:

> Concerning the coming of our Lord Jesus Christ and our being gathered to him, we ask you, brothers, not to become easily unsettled or alarmed by some prophecy, report or letter supposed to have come from us, saying that the day of the Lord has already come. Don't let anyone deceive you in any way, for that day will not come until the rebellion occurs and the man of lawlessness is revealed, the man doomed to destruction.

Paul seems to indicate that there will be an intensified apostasy, a falling away, a rebellion, which will take place before the parousia, and that this will be associated with the man of lawlessness being revealed. Actually, the definite article is there, in verse 3. He refers to it as the *apostasia*, the apostasy, a final climatic apostasy, the culmination of what is already beginning to happen. 'For the secret power of lawlessness is already at work; but the one who holds it back will continue to do so till he is taken out of the way' (2 Thessalonians 2:7).

Like the distress, this sign of apostasy is evident throughout the period of the last days, but it comes to its climatic form just before the parousia. And we are helped by the further revelation through Paul, which explains why Jesus taught the disciples to regard that as one of the great signs. Those who fall away will be at least outwardly associated with the people of God, and who is to say that the empty churches of the Western world and the way in which our culture has turned its back upon Christ is not the *apostasia* which he talks about, the sign of his coming? While we cannot be sure of this, we do live in a time of great falling away.

And the third sign that he gives is the sign of the *antichrist*. Like the first two signs, there are Old Testament antecedents to this and Jesus draws attention to them particularly, when he refers to the prophecy of Daniel. **'So when you see standing in the holy place "the abomination that causes desolation," spoken of through the prophet Daniel – let the reader understand –** (obviously this is a comment of Jesus about reading Daniel, not about reading Matthew's Gospel) **then let those who are in Judea flee to the mountains'** (24:15-16). In its context, Daniel 11:36, which has that phrase 'the abomination that causes desolation' refers to a king of the north who will exalt himself against God and proclaim himself to be greater than the Lord. Almost all evangelical commentaries tell us that this was fulfilled in Antiochus Epiphanes, who desecrated the Jerusalem temple and who demanded to be worshipped as God. He dedicated the temple to Zeus and offered pig sacrifices on the altar; in fact, he placed a pagan altar on top of the altar of burnt offering in the temple. When Jesus said these words, they had already been fulfilled, but he picks up that prophecy and shows that it has only been partially fulfilled and that there is another horizon beyond. Within a generation, the Roman legions under Titus would march into the holy city and place their standards depicting the images of the 'divine' Caesar in the Lord's temple. At that point those who lived in Judah should flee to the mountains.

It is the presence, in the place of holiness, of that which is antichrist, 'the abomination that causes desolation', the exaltation of humanity in opposition and rebellion against God, that Jesus says is a mark of the sign of his coming. We noted in 2 Thessalonians the reference to the 'man of lawlessness' whom Paul describes further: 'He will oppose and will exalt himself over everything that is called God or is worshipped, so that he sets himself up in God's temple, proclaiming himself to be God' (2 Thessalonians 2:4). Does that not give special point to Matthew 24:23-24: **'At that time if anyone says to you, "Look here is the Christ!", or, "There he is!" do not believe it. For false Christs and false prophets will appear and perform great signs and miracles** (as will the man of lawlessness), **to deceive even the elect - if that is possible.'** Some will even claim to be the Christ. 2 Thessalonians 2:9 tells us that 'the coming of the lawless one will be in accordance with the work of Satan - displayed in all kinds of counterfeit miracles, signs and wonders, and in every sort of evil that deceives those who are perishing.' So, the New Testament does seem to indicate that while antichrists are going to be characteristic of the whole period of the last days, in the last last days, there will be an intensification of the opposition and rebellion before the return of the Lord.

All this means is that these three great signs are given, not to encourage speculation or to enable us to date the parousia (that is never the point of New Testament eschatology), but to prepare us for the event. Similarly, the signs of God's judgment in 24:6-8, 'wars, rumours of wars, nation against nation, kingdom against kingdom, famines, earthquakes,' as Jesus says in verse 8, **are the beginning of birth pains**. They are signs that occur throughout the last days.

Our understanding of such tragedies of human experience must surely be taken from Jesus' teaching in Luke 13:1-5. There Jesus deals with two recent horrors a massacre of Galilean worshippers by Pilate and the collapse of a tower in Siloam, which killed eighteen people. It was not that these people were worse sinners than others, or more guilty before God, he says, 'but unless you repent, you too will all perish.' These are reminders that we live in an uncertain, finite world. Our own lives and the world in which we live them will both come to an end. Death is the ultimate statistic, since one in one dies! But they are also manifestations of a world already under the wrath of God in judgment and it is only because of his mercy that we are not all consumed, in a moment.

Nevertheless, such sufferings are also the beginning of birth pains, the sign of new life, the beginning of something better in the fullness of the kingdom, the Messianic banquet that is yet to be. The signs point to the end and provide a constant reminder and pledge that the end will undoubtedly come, as verses 30-31 clearly and vividly state: **'At that time the sign of the Son of Man will appear in the sky, and all the nations of the earth will mourn. They will see the Son of Man coming on the clouds of the sky, with power and great glory. And he will send his angels with a loud trumpet call, and they will gather his elect from the four winds, from one end of the heavens to the other.'**

One of the reasons why the disciples are not to be misled by false signs is that the real event will not be able to be missed. The natural upheavals which verse 29 speaks about herald the appearance of the king's ensign in the sky and the sounding of the king's trumpet, as he gathers his elect from heaven and from the 'round earth's imagined corners'. As far as the timing is concerned we are simply instructed to read the parable of the fig tree (verse 32), and recognise that just as the fall of Jerusalem happened within the generation to whom Jesus was speaking, so the signs of the immediacy of the parousia will be witnessed by the same generation that will experience the event. Therefore, Jesus is calling his church in every generation to be ready for that momentous event to take place.

Ready for the Master's return

From verse 36 onwards, the focus shifts from the fact of the coming, and the signs of it which we are to recognise, to the need to be ready. Remarkably, the emphasis in four of the five parables which follow next is on the delay of the coming. It is extraordinary, how Jesus can be accused of having got his eschatology wrong, when he so clearly warns that the parousia will not be imminent, that there will actually be a protracted delay!

The first four parables make this one point in different ways, again and again. In 24:43-44, it is the story of the thief at night. It will be a sudden coming, Jesus says, but that does not mean it will be soon. We are not to try to read the signs in such a generalized way that we are encouraged to put off our responsibility to be ready for the great day. Rather, they should motivate us to live today in the light of his coming. In fact, the longer the coming is delayed the more likely we are to be taken by surprise. So, Jesus warns us, **'you also must be ready'** (verse 44). He will come at an hour when we are not expecting him. That alone ought to have stopped the nonsense of speculation about dates, which has so often plagued the church and made this doctrine the province of cranks and eccentrics, bringing its essential teaching into disrepute. As the year 2000 comes up on the horizon we can expect an explosion of eschatological excitement, just as there was at the first millennium, and we shall need to keep cool Biblical heads and warm expectant hearts in the midst of it all.

The second parable, 24:45-51, is about the disorderly servants, who presume on their master's delay. Because it is so long, they think it is going to be permanent. So, they indulge in all sorts of selfish behaviour and faithlessness, and then suddenly the master returns, judges and punishes them. '**He will cut him to pieces and assign him a place with the hypocrites, where there will be weeping and gnashing of teeth.**'

In 25:1-13, the parable of the virgins turns on the delay being unexpectedly long. It is going to take a long time for the king to come. Given human nature, that will lead to carelessness and lack of adequate preparation. The parable teaches us that readiness for the coming of the bridegroom cannot be transferred and it cannot be shared; it is an individual responsibility. It is a parable of personal accountability.

In the same way, the fourth parable about the talents, 25:14-30, hinges on delay: '**After a long time the master of those servants returned and settled accounts with them**' (verse 19). It is a delay in which the servants are tested, not only on the performance of their duty, but on the investment of their talents, on their loyalty and love for the master. And of course, the lazy servant has a completely wrong view of the master: '**I was afraid and went out and hid your talent**' (verse 25).

This issue which Jesus is posing is very clear. How is the church going to cope with the delay and use the time constructively? It will be a sudden coming, but we must not use the fact of the delay for our own selfish faithlessness, by failing to be ready, by not using our talents, or by saying it's not worth it. Every day counts. In each of those parables, there is a moment of reckoning. There is a point of judgment at which an assessment, a division is made. One night the house is broken into. One night the master returns. Eventually the bridegroom arrives. And what has gone on during the delay determines the judgment. That much is clear in the last parable of the sheep and the goats, as well. But at that point the widely conflicting interpretations begin. Yet this last parable is clearly the climax of the discourse, and in some senses the climax of all five teaching blocks. The Sermon on the Mount ends with separation: '**By your fruit you will recognise them.**' '**Not everyone who says to me, Lord, Lord,**

will enter the kingdom, but only he who does the will of my Father' (7:20-27) The parables in chapter 13 end with separation - the good fish are collected in baskets and the bad fish drawn in by the dragnet are thrown away. So here, this teaching block also ends with separation, the separation of the sheep from the goats, with eternal consequences, and the verdict of that day depends on what has gone on previously up to the point of the parousia, when the Son of Man comes in his glory (verse 31). In other words, the judgment of the last day is in fact a judgment according to works.

That assertion of course undergirds the liberal scholars' case for interpreting the parable of the sheep and the goats, according to what has come to be called the 'social gospel'. It is commonly said that in this parable of the sheep and of the goats, we have a statement of the grounds on which we are going to be judged at the last day: **'For I was hungry and you gave me something to eat, I was thirsty and you gave me something to drink, I was a stranger and you invited me in'** and so on (verses 35, 36). Our attitude to Christ is determined then by the extent and manner in which we have carried out these humanitarian acts, and his attitude to us will reciprocate that. This is the interpretation of the parable. If that is right, then of course we should spend our greatest energy in pursuing those ends. If those are actually the things that are going to justify us before God, if that is how we serve Christ, then those are the things that ought to be of primary importance to us. It is a widely held interpretation and not all evangelical commentators want to challenge it. One of them, for example, says, 'There is one test and one only of the extent of our love for Christ, and it is a very uncomfortable one: How have we handled the poor?'

But this presents us with a major problem, for if this is what the parable really means, that we are accepted by Christ on the grounds of our good deeds, it would seem flatly to contradict the rest of the New Testament, with its teaching that salvation is through faith in God's grace, demonstrated in the atoning death of Christ on the cross, and in that alone. There would seem then to be two areas of confusion which we need to clarify. The first is a confusion about faith and works and the second about the exegesis of this parable.

There is an undeniably clear strand of New Testament teaching that the final judgment will be according to works. We have seen it in Matthew 7:21, 'Not those who say to me, "Lord, Lord", but those who do the will of my Father who is in heaven.' We can see it in Matthew 16:27, 'The Son of Man is going to come in his Father's glory with his angels, and then he will reward each person according to what he has done.' Nor is it only in Matthew. In Romans 2:6, where Paul is quoting Psalm 62, he says, 'God will give to each person according to what he has done', and right at the end of the Bible, in Revelation 22:12, 'Behold I am coming soon. My reward is with me, and I will give to everyone according to what he has done.'

This strand is important because it establishes the close connection between faith and works. But salvation is always by faith and never earned by works. So Calvin comments: 'It is faith alone which justifies and yet the faith which justifies is not alone.' That is also the argument of James in his letter. Faith must reveal itself in works, and such works are the fruit, the evidence, of a true faith. So the judgment about works is actually a judgment about faith, because the reality of faith is seen in the evidence of the works. The works are the mark, externally, of the inner reality of faith. Hence the emphasis in Matthew on fruit and the comments about God's disappointment with the old Israel, that they are not fruitful. If the faith is genuine, works will be there. If they are not, then the faith is not real. So the works are a part of that judgment.

If we have got that balance right, then we can take a more careful look at the text in Matthew 25 and try to exegete it properly. The subjects of the judgment (verse 32) are all the nations, that is the Gentile, heathen nations, as the Jews would have described them, those who were as yet unreached by the gospel of Christ, when Christ told this story. From among these Gentile nations, the shepherd separates sheep from goats. Jesus is saying to the Jews that it is not Israel who are the sheep and the Gentiles the goats, though that is what the Pharisees would have taught. Rather, from the Gentile nations, there will be those who are revealed to be his sheep. Then, the decision about their final destiny is given in verse 34: **Then the King will say to those on his right, "Come, you who are blessed by my Father; take your inheritance, the kingdom prepared for you since the creation of the world."**

Clearly, then, this judgment is not an investigation of the lives of the sheep to see that they have done enough good to earn a place in heaven - quite the reverse. The sheep have merited nothing. They are objects of the Father's favour and grace. Furthermore, they inherit the kingdom, not as a reward that is earned, but as a gift that is received. Indeed, this kingdom has been prepared for them, Jesus says, before they were ever given life, before the creation of the world. So the choice of them was based on grace before they even existed, before there could be any sort of merit. Verses 35 and 36 actually explain the reasons for this decision. It is based on their attitude to the king, to Christ himself. The sheep have illustrated their reception of Christ by their actions, just as the goats later on illustrate their rejection of Christ by their lack of action. Notice too that this is apparently a great surprise to the sheep. The righteous answer (verse 37), **'Lord, when did we see you hungry, and feed you ...'** and so on. Clearly, they were not doing these things hoping to earn eternal life by their good works. Their works were the evidence of the faith in Christ that they were exercising, and they seem to have been largely unconscious of them.

Verse 40 provides the explanation. **The King will reply, "I tell you the truth, whatever you did for the one of the least of these brothers of mine, you did it for me."** Who are these 'brothers of mine'? Matthew's Gospel has made it very clear. They are those who **'do the will of my Father'** (12:49-50). They are disciples. So just as the Son always did the things which pleased the Father, the brothers and sisters related to him in the family of God, in their devotion and discipleship, are committed to the Father's will, and the elaboration of that comes in the second part of the parable. **'I tell you the truth, whatever you did not do for one of the least of these, you did not do for me'** (verse 45). It is very reminiscent of the 'little ones' in chapter 18, or the cup of cold water being given in the Lord's name in chapter 10, which is not without its reward. In 23:8 he has defined as brothers those who submit to him as their one Master, and who belong to the one Father in heaven. In 28:10 the risen Lord will appear to the woman hurrying away from the tomb, with the command, **'Go and tell my brothers to go to Galilee: there they will see me.'**

Just a few verses later, as if to put the matter beyond all dispute, Matthew tells us, **Then the eleven disciples went to Galilee, to the**

mountain where Jesus had told them to go (28:16).

The judgment is of all the nations, because from all the nations the new Israel will be constituted. There will be those who are Jews by race as well as those who are Gentiles found among the sheep of God's flock on that last day, but the old days of Jewish priority and privilege have gone, in the gospel. All the world is now on level ground before the God of the whole earth. All the world is to be judged on the basis of their relationship to Christ, which is revealed in how they have behaved towards his people. As Dr Don Carson expresses it, 'Good deeds done to Jesus' followers, even the least of them, are not only works of compassion and morality, but reflect where people stand in relation to the kingdom and to Jesus himself.' The basis of the judgment is how we have treated Christ, and the parable presents such a test of that as to eliminate the very possibility of hypocrisy. The way to be ready for the coming of the king is to be active, showing our love to Christ's brothers, and as his brothers to be proclaiming the message of his kingship by our lives and by our lips.

The conclusion

With that awesome thrust at the end of Christ's teaching, the Gospel moves to its climax in the ultimate confrontation between the rebellious human race and its Creator. Matthew documents the depravity of human sinfulness very faithfully in the next few chapters. In 26:4, the chief priests and elders meet with Caiaphas **and they plotted to arrest Jesus in some sly way and kill him.** In 26:59, they are **looking for false evidence against Jesus so that they could put him to death.** As, later, Jesus stands before Pontius Pilate, at the accusation of those religious leaders, Matthew tells us that Pilate **knew it was out of envy that they had handed Jesus over to him** (27:18). When Pilate offers to release Jesus, it is the chief priests and elders who persuade **the crowd to ask for Barabbas and to have Jesus executed** (27:20). But it is at the cross itself that the full version of their implacable hatred is revealed in their scurrilous mocking of the Lord from heaven: **'He saved others,' they said, 'but he can't save himself! He's the King of Israel! Let him come down now from the cross, and we will believe in him. He trusts in God. Let God rescue him now if he wants him, for he said, "I am the Son of God!" '**

(27:42-43). Saviour, King of Israel, Son of God – every one of his most fundamental fulfilment claims is taken, trampled on and thrown back into his teeth. But the irony is intensely moving. It is precisely because he has come to save others that he will not save himself. It was as his own people rejected his sonship, that the Gentile guards, seeing all that had happened, came to the conclusion, **'Surely he was the Son of God!'** (27:54).

At the death of the Lord Jesus Christ, at the very moment when he gave up his spirit, **the curtain of the temple was torn in two from top to bottom** (27:51). The barrier which had existed since first the people of Israel had trembled at the foot of Mount Sinai as the Lord descended in smoke and fire, and which had been expressed in the thick curtain which separated the worshipper from the presence of God from the day the tabernacle was erected - that barrier was once and for all removed. God was saying to all the world, to whosoever will, 'You can come in now.' All that the Old Testament types foreshadowed, all that the law demanded, has been fulfilled in the life and death of the Son of God.

The short, concluding chapter of Matthew's Gospel is masterly. First, there is the historical evidence of the empty tomb and glorious assertion that Christ is alive: **'He is not here; he has risen, just as he said'** (28:6). But in the face of this total victory over all the hostile powers that were ranged against him, what is happening to the Jewish leaders? We find they are still at their old business, unbelieving, rebellious, full of lies, bribing the guards, spreading stories about how the disciples had come and stolen the body away (28:12-15).

So, what about the new Israel? We find the eleven meeting the risen Lord in Galilee and **When they saw him, they worshipped him; but some doubted** (28:17). How refreshingly true and honest that is! But the Gospel ends with the God, who tore the curtain down to allow his disciples to come into his presence, commissioning this bewildered, uncertain group of followers to go out from his presence into all the nations, to make disciples. Their authority is delegated to them by the Lord to whom all authority belongs. Their message is to teach disciples from all the nations to obey all that he has commanded them. Their promise and enabling is that the risen Lord will be with them always, **'to the very end of the age'** (28:18-20).

We find ourselves so many centuries later, with so much church history good and bad behind us, in that concluding verse. For it is not yet the end of the age, and the promise is to all who go at his command, *always*, until the end of time. The Gospel that began with Emmanuel, God with us, in the birth of the child (1:23) ends with Emmanuel, God with us, as we go to preach Christ to the ends of the earth, until the end of the age. What he has fulfilled, we must now proclaim. That is how we take Jesus seriously.

Footnotes

1. D A Carson in 'Matthew' in vol. 8 of *The Expositor's Bible Commentary*, Zondervan, 1984, page 130.
2. John Bright, *The Authority of the Old Testament*, Baker Books, 1967.
3. D A Carson *op. cit.* page 130.
4. I. Howard Marshall in article on 'Church' in the Dictionary of Jesus and the Gospels (ed. J.B. Green and S. McKnight), Inter-Varsity Press, Leicester, 1992, p. 123.
5. D A Carson *op. cit.*, page 401.
6. David F. Wells, *No Place For Truth*, Eerdmans, Grand Rapids. 1993 (pages 279-280)
7. D A Carson *op. cit.* page 520.